MW00565549

CHAMPIONS

AGAIN

THE STORY OF THE PATRIOTS FOURTH NFL CHAMPIONSHIP

Sean Leahy, Sports Editor

Mark J. Murphy, Deputy Sports Editor

Bill McIlwrath, Night Sports Editor

James Potter, Managing Editor Production

Jim Mahoney, Photo Editor

Ted Ancher, Assistant Photo Editor

Boston Herald Photo Staff

Martha Reagan, Head Librarian

* * *

Patrick J. Purcell, Publisher

Joseph Sciacca, Editor In Chief

Gwen Gage, VP/Promotion and Marketing

Ty Adamson, Senior Designer

Jennifer Morse, VP/ Digital Operations

Betsy Kane, Digital Operations Specialist

Copy Editors

Jim Clark

Paul Sullivan

Jim Lazar

Karl Zerfoss

Chris Letourneau

Michael Kilduff

Mike Biglin

Jon Couture

Mike Trainor

Bill Corey

Nate Dow

Vinnie Pullia

Bruce Castleberry

Andy Silva

KCI SPORTS PUBLISHING

Peter J. Clark, Publisher
Molly Voorheis, Managing Editor
Nicky Brillowski, Book and Cover Design
Sam Schmidt, Advertising

© 2015 Boston Herald
All rights reserved. Except for use in a review, the reproduction or
utilization of this work in any form or by any electronic, mechanical, or other means,
now known or hereafter invented, including xerography, photocopying, and recording,
and in any information storage and retrieval system, is forbidden without the
written permission of the publisher.

ISBN: 978-1-940056-19-7

Printed in the United States of America
KCI Sports Publishing   3340 Whiting Avenue, Suite 5   Stevens Point, WI 54481
Phone: 1-800-697-3756   Fax: 715-344-2668
www.kcisports.com

This is an unofficial publication. This book is in no way affiliated with, licensed by or endorsed
by the National Football League or the New England Patriots.

CONTENTS

Patriots quarterback Tom Brady gets a hug from head coach Bill Belichick after beating the Seahawks in the Super Bowl.
By Matt West / Boston Herald

Patriots quarterback Tom Brady unloads early under pressure from Seattle Seahawks defensive end Michael Bennett.
By Matt West / Boston Herald

INTRODUCTION

Congratulations to the Patriots for all their success in winning Super Bowl XLIX and providing fans across New England with a season full of thrilling memories.

It was our privilege at the Herald to cover this season from training camp in July until the confetti fell in Glendale on Feb. 1.

Our team of writers, photographers, editors and others who pull together our coverage were happy to provide readers with unique access, analysis and insight that isn't available anywhere else. We're delighted to be able to lift the curtain for readers on what turned out to be a remarkable Patriots season.

From capturing Rob Gronkowski's touchdown spikes to breaking down how it all came together for the Patriots — including documenting some of their bumps along the road there — we are confident the Herald provided the best possible coverage of the Patriots this season.

I know you'll enjoy the memories of a wonderful season we expect this book to provide. And we hope to be able to do the same thing next year.

Sincerely,

Purcell

Patrick J. Purcell
Publisher

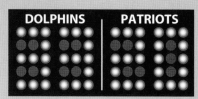

DOLPHINS | **PATRIOTS**

REGULAR SEASON > GAME 1

Sept. 7, 2014

PATRIOTS @ DOLPHINS

MANGLED IN MIAMI

Patriots get run over in second half

By JEFF HOWE | *Boston Herald*

The Patriots needed a floodlight to showcase everything they had going for them after a tremendous offseason and training camp. It seemed only a microscope was necessary to reveal their perceived weaknesses. Credit the Miami Dolphins for having the vision to exploit those areas with a thorough 33-20 win at Sun Life Stadium. And when it really mattered, the Dolphins outscored the visitors 23-0 in a one-sided second half.

The Patriots are now in sole possession of last place in the AFC East for the first time since Tom Brady took over as starting quarterback in 2001, and they've got a losing record for the second time in a decade.

"It's not how you start (the season)," nose tackle Vince Wilfork said. "It's how you finish. We started (crappy), I'll tell you that, but we'll get it together."

It started with the offensive line, which allowed four sacks and countless hits on Brady. He completed 29-of-56 passes for 249 yards and one touchdown, but he was only 10-of-27 for 62 yards in the second half, when he also lost two fumbles in Patriots territory.

The offensive line was tabbed as the biggest question mark, as 60 percent of its starters weren't known until kickoff. Starters Nate Solder, Marcus Cannon, Dan Connolly, Jordan Devey and Sebastian Vollmer and rotational center Ryan Wendell couldn't keep Brady upright long enough to find anyone down the field after halftime. This follows the decision to trade Logan Mankins to the Tampa Bay Buccaneers.

"You can look for Logan all you want. He's not coming back," Vollmer said when asked if they missed Mankins' leadership. "I just don't see it that way. I don't know what to tell you."

Even the ever-reliable tight end Michael Hoomanawanui whiffed on the Dolphins' Cameron Wake before the speedy rusher forced Brady's first fumble in the third quarter, setting up Ryan Tannehill's 14-yard touchdown pass to Mike

Patriots quarterback Tom Brady is sacked in the third quarter by Miami Dolphins linebacker Chris McCain with the help of Jared Odrick.

By Matt West / Boston Herald

Miami Dolphins linebacker Jelani Jenkins and free safety Louis Delmas break up a fourth-quarter pass intended for Patriots tight end Timothy Wright.

By Matt West / Boston Herald

Wallace that tied the game, 20-20.

The Pats followed with a three-and-out that led to a 10-play drive, which Miami capped with Caleb Sturgis' 22-yard field goal that gave them a 23-20 advantage with 2:38 remaining in the third quarter. At that point, the Dolphins had 13 third-quarter points to the Patriots' seven offensive snaps.

"You can't play the way we played today and think we'll win a game this season," Brady said. "There's nothing positive to really take from the things we were doing."

Not even tight end Rob Gronkowski could help the cause. He caught four passes for 40 yards and a 6-yard touchdown that put the Pats ahead, 17-7, in the second quarter, but the Patriots limited his playing time in the second half. Gronkowski only played two of 20 offensive snaps while the Dolphins turned a 20-10 deficit into a 30-20 lead, and he wasn't targeted a single time.

But the Patriots still had their chances despite their offensive ineptitude after the defense forced back-to-back three-and-outs. Yet, Brady

Patriots punter Ryan Allen gets his first quarter punt blocked by Miami Dolphins linebacker Chris McCain.
By Matt West / Boston Herald

GAME STATISTICS

	New England	10	10	0	0	—	20
	Miami	7	3	13	10	—	33

FIRST QUARTER

MIA	TD	11:46	Lamar Miller 4 Yd pass from Ryan Tannehill (Caleb Sturgis Kick) **Drive:** 4 plays, 15 yds, 1:50
NE	TD	5:10	Shane Vereen 2 Yd Run (Stephen Gostkowski Kick) **Drive:** 13 plays, 80 yds, 6:36
NE	FG	0:47	Stephen Gostkowski 47 Yd Field Goal **Drive:** 7 plays, 6 yds, 2:52

SECOND QUARTER

NE	TD	8:37	Rob Gronkowski 6 Yd pass from Tom Brady (Stephen Gostkowski Kick) **Drive:** 11 plays, 94 yds, 4:19
MIA	FG	1:59	Caleb Sturgis 38 Yd Field Goal **Drive:** 11 plays, 55 yds, 4:25
NE	FG	0:06	Stephen Gostkowski 45 Yd Field Goal **Drive:** 8 plays, 47 yds, 1:53

THIRD QUARTER

MIA	FG	10:46	Caleb Sturgis 24 Yd Field Goal **Drive:** 8 plays, 66 yds, 4:14
MIA	TD	6:55	Mike Wallace 14 Yd pass from Ryan Tannehill (Caleb Sturgis Kick) **Drive:** 4 plays, 34 yds, 2:04
MIA	FG	2:38	Caleb Sturgis 22 Yd Field Goal **Drive:** 10 plays, 50 yds, 3:15

FOURTH QUARTER

MIA	TD	3:29	Knowshon Moreno 4 Yd Run (Caleb Sturgis Kick) **Drive:** 12 plays, 85 yds, 6:01
MIA	FG	2:44	Caleb Sturgis 27 Yd Field Goal **Drive:** 4 plays, 5 yds, 0:20

couldn't hit wide receiver Julian Edelman (six receptions, 95 yards) on a deep double-move up the left side on third-and-9 with 9:56 remaining.

The Dolphins buried the Pats on the next series, and they seemed all the more helpless while cornerback Darrelle Revis was restricted to the sideline with cramps in his left leg. Knowshon Moreno (24 carries, 134 yards) and Lamar Miller (11-59) combined to rush seven times for 29 yards on the drive, and they converted all three third-down bids, including Moreno's 4-yard touchdown run after sliding through Wilfork's tackle attempt in the backfield. Even while Tannehill struggled, the Patriots couldn't clog the running lanes.

Brady went to the air three times while faced with a 30-20 deficit, but attempts to running back Shane Vereen, receiver Brandon LaFell and Gronkowski hit the ground harmlessly. Wake then exploded past Vollmer to force Brady's second fumble on fourth down and stifle their last meaningful opportunity. The Pats only had two first downs in their first six possessions of the second half after moving the chains 15 times

before the break.

"Our execution was just terrible," Brady said after the second season-opening loss of his career.

"We can't hold our heads down," Wilfork said. "It's a long season. We definitely have to get better. We will get better."■

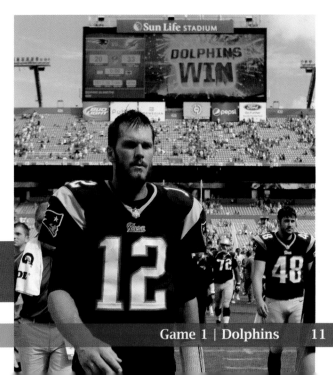

New England Patriots quarterback Tom Brady walks off the field dejected after the Patriots are upset by the Miami Dolphins.
By Matt West / Boston Herald

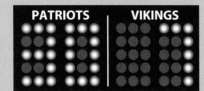

SLAM ON THE LAKES

Pats pick apart Minn. for 1st win

By JEFF HOWE | *Boston Herald*

The Patriots dumped last week's playbook into one of Minnesota's 10,000 lakes, and the widespread adjustments helped them sink the Vikings, 30-7, at TCF Bank Stadium.

Their greatest failures in the season-opening loss to the Dolphins were flipped into strengths as the Patriots evened up their record with a thorough beating of the hosts.

"We knew we were capable of it," defensive tackle Vince Wilfork said. "I have no clue what happened last week. But at the same time, after that game, I was disappointed, but I had the confidence we were going to get fixed whatever we needed to get fixed because we were too good of a defense to look like that."

Quarterback Tom Brady stayed relatively clean behind the same offensive line, and his only sack occurred in the fourth quarter when the outcome had long since been decided. With the luxury of remaining upright, Brady completed 15-of-22 passes for 149 yards and one touchdown, and he was particularly efficient targeting wide receiver Julian Edelman (six receptions, 81 yards, touchdown) and tight end Rob Gronkowski (four catches, 32 yards).

"I am glad we won," a surprisingly dissatisfied Brady said. "It was a great team win. A lot of guys contributed. A lot of great plays were made."

Defensively, they finally looked like the shutdown unit that's been touted for much of the offseason. Darrelle Revis intercepted his first pass and only allowed one 4-yard reception to receiver Greg Jennings on the six times the cornerback was targeted by quarterback Matt Cassel. Safety Devin McCourty, cornerback Logan Ryan and defensive lineman Dominique Easley joined Revis in the Cassel pick party.

Patriots running back Stevan Ridley heads upfield against the Minnesota Vikings.
By Nancy Lane / Boston Herald

Patriots defensive tackle Dominique Easley (R) celebrates his fourth-quarter interception with his teammates.
By Nancy Lane / Boston Herald

The defense worked in cohesion, too, as end Chandler Jones (two sacks), linebacker Dont'a Hightower (two sacks), end Rob Ninkovich (sack) and cornerback Kyle Arrington (strip sack) harassed Cassel a week after they struggled to finish the job against Dolphins quarterback Ryan Tannehill. The Pats also held the Adrian Peterson-less cast of Vikings to 54 rushing yards on 19 carries, shoring up a front that wasn't competitive in Miami.

"We were making plays everywhere today," Revis said. "We played great team ball today."

The recovery operation didn't exactly start well, as they allowed former Patriots quarterback Cassel (19-of-36, 202 yards, touchdown) to breeze down the field and take advantage of a couple of blown coverages. The most damning led to fullback Matt Asiata's 25-yard touchdown catch and a 7-0 Minnesota lead.

McCourty sparked the comeback, tracking down a deep bid for receiver Jarius Wright and returning the interception to the Vikings 1-yard line. Running back Stevan Ridley, the benefactor of a refocused ground attack with 25 carries for 101 yards, tied the score two plays later.

After kicker Stephen Gostkowski's 48-yard field goal made it 10-7, Revis jumped Jennings' route for his first pick with the Pats. Brady finished the job on the next series, finding Edelman for 44 yards on third-and-14 and then hanging in the pocket to take a wicked hit while delivering a 9-yard fade to Edelman for the touchdown and 17-7 advantage.

Jones put it out of reach from there. After Cassel missed speedy receiver Cordarrelle Patterson (four receptions, 56 yards) for a potential 30-yard touchdown, Jones broke through the line to smother a field goal attempt and returned the block 58 yards for a 24-7 lead before halftime.

The Patriots, who blew a 10-point halftime lead against the Dolphins, stifled the Vikings after the break. The Vikings only registered three first downs in five second-half possessions before the Pats removed Revis for the final series, and the Patriots displayed a closing instinct that wasn't present in the opening defeat. Gostkowski converted a 47-yarder and 27-yarder to cap the scoring.

They knew they were capable of this type of performance, and they proved it to themselves with a convincing win after such an uncertain display in Week 1.

"We want to play great football," Revis said. "I think that says the word. It sums it up. We just want to play great football, and we did a great job today. We've just got to keep on building off this game. Going into next week, we have a home game against Oakland, and just ride that momentum into that game." ∎

Patriots strong safety Devin McCourty just misses a pick 6 as he gets knocked out of bounds by Minnesota Vikings tackle Matt Kalil after an interception.

By Nancy Lane / Boston Herald

GAME STATISTICS		New England	10	14	3	3	—	30
		Miami	7	0	0	0	—	7

FIRST QUARTER

MIN TD 10:54 Matt Asiata 25 Yd pass from Matt Cassel (Blair Walsh Kick)
Drive: 7 plays, 80 yds, 4:06

NE TD 6:14 Stevan Ridley 1 Yd Run (Stephen Gostkowski Kick)
Drive: 2 plays, 1 yds, 0:43

NE FG 0:32 Stephen Gostkowski 48 Yd Field Goal
Drive: 10 plays, 40 yds, 4:11

SECOND QUARTER

NE TD 9:30 Julian Edelman 9 Yd pass from Tom Brady (Stephen Gostkowski Kick)
Drive: 7 plays, 61 yds, 4:00

NE TD 0:09 Chandler Jones 58 Yd Return of Blocked Field Goal (Stephen Gostkowski Kick)
Drive: 11 plays, 52 yds, 2:49

THIRD QUARTER

NE FG 8:32 Stephen Gostkowski 47 Yd Field Goal
Drive: 5 plays, 17 yds, 1:10

FOURTH QUARTER

NE FG 14:57 Stephen Gostkowski 27 Yd Field Goal
Drive: 11 plays, 46 yds, 6:49

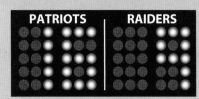

WILFORK ISLAND

Defensive lineman saves day in Patriots home opener

By JEFF HOWE | *Boston Herald*

After successfully targeting cornerback Darrelle Revis for much of the day, Raiders quarterback Derek Carr found himself stranded on a more formidable island.

Defensive lineman Vince Wilfork snagged a surprising interception in the red zone yesterday to preserve the Patriots' 16-9 victory in the home opener at Gillette Stadium. After setting themselves up for an unlikely disaster throughout the game, the Patriots escaped in an equally inexplicable fashion with Wilfork's hands securing a batted ball and the win.

"It was great," Revis said. "They're calling him Wilfork Island now."

Revis allowed Carr to complete 5-of-6 passes for 63 yards in his direction, and he was also pinned for a negated pass interference penalty. It was an out-of-body experience for an aptly-nicknamed corner who held QBs Ryan Tannehill and Matt Cassel to 3-of-11 passes for 40 yards, one touchdown and one interception in the previous two games.

But that's nitpicking for a defense that held back-to-back opponents to fewer than 10 points, and the unit is a major reason why the Pats (2-1) have a winning record heading into a Monday Night Football showdown with the Chiefs.

Still, the defense wasn't proud of its performance. After all, it allowed Carr (21-of-34, 174 yards, interception) to march down the field to nearly tie the game in the final minute of the fourth quarter. Running back Darren McFadden (18 carries, 59 yards) thought he had evened the contest with a 6-yard touchdown, but it was called back due to left guard Gabe Jackson's holding penalty. On the next play, a pass to receiver Denarius Moore bounced off his hands and then off cornerback Logan Ryan before settling into Wilfork's meaty mitts at the 10.

"What I mean by ugly," Revis said while explaining his

Patriots wide receiver Julian Edelman tries to leap over the Oakland Raiders strong safety Usama Young.

By Matt West / Boston Herald

description of the game, "it's not the way we wanted it to go. The game, how it was today, I don't think any team wants it to go that way. It was an ugly win, flags everywhere, execution-wise. It was an ugly win. The thing we can take out of this game is we had great character. Guys stuck into the game through all four quarters, and we played hard."

Quarterback Tom Brady (24-of-37, 234 yards, touchdown) and the Pats' inconsistent offense can thank Wilfork and company for the bailout. This time, the most egregious mistakes occurred in the red zone, where the Patriots were held to three Stephen Gostkowski field goals (21, 20, 36) on four visits.

The sole conversion came in the second quarter after Brady called a timeout at the line of scrimmage that might have been designed to get Rob Gronkowski on the field for a key third-and-2 from the 6. Gronkowski, who had his best statistical game of the season with three catches for 44 yards, emerged after the respite and beat the defense on a drag route to give the Pats a 7-3 advantage.

Patriots wide receiver Julian Edelman makes a 15-yard reception despite having Oakland Raiders cornerback Carlos Rogers in his face in the fourth quarter.
By Nancy Lane / Boston Herald

GAME STATISTICS

	Oakland	3	0	6	0	—	9
	New England	0	10	0	6	—	16

FIRST QUARTER

OAK   FG   4:37   Sebastian Janikowski 49 Yd Field Goal
Drive: 13 plays, 50 yds, 6:10

SECOND QUARTER

NE   TD   4:14   Rob Gronkowski 6 Yd pass from Tom Brady (Stephen Gostkowski Kick)
Drive: 15 plays, 84 yds, 6:43

NE   FG   0:00   Stephen Gostkowski 21 Yd Field Goal
Drive: 10 plays, 48 yds, 2:45

THIRD QUARTER

OAK   FG   9:39   Sebastian Janikowski 37 Yd Field Goal
Drive: 7 plays, 29 yds, 3:13

OAK   FG   2:21   Sebastian Janikowski 47 Yd Field Goal
Drive: 9 plays, 57 yds, 3:48

FOURTH QUARTER

NE   FG   13:42   Stephen Gostkowski 20 Yd Field Goal
Drive: 10 plays, 57 yds, 3:39

NE   FG   6:20   Stephen Gostkowski 36 Yd Field Goal
Drive: 12 plays, 63 yds, 4:55

Patriots tight end Rob Gronkowski spikes the ball after he scores a touchdown.

By Matt West / Boston Herald

Before the half, the Pats had a first-and-goal from the 3 but managed a 1-yard run from running back Stevan Ridley (19 carries, 54 yards) before running back Shane Vereen rushed for no gain and center Dan Connolly's low third-down snap forced Brady to chuck it to the sideline to preserve enough time for Gostkowski's field goal and a 10-3 lead.

Brady nearly was decapitated in the first two series in the third quarter, as right guard Jordan Devey was beat by defensive lineman Justin Tuck for a third-down sack, and left tackle Nate Solder was dusted by linebacker Khalil Mack, who bended Brady's spine on a later third-down incompletion.

But when the Pats finally returned to the red zone, thanks in large part to one of receiver Julian Edelman's 10 catches for 84 yards, they faltered on first-and-goal from the 2. Vereen (11 touches, 37 yards) was stuffed for no gain again, and

Gronkowski and receiver Danny Amendola couldn't corral Brady's next two passes. Gostkowski's 20-yarder made it 13-9 with 13:42 remaining in the fourth quarter, and his 36-yard boot pushed it to 16-9 with 6:20 to go.

With one more chance to put it away, the offense could only construct a three-and-out that was lowlighted by a second sack of Brady that led to a long-shot, third-and-17 situation. Those mistakes were frequent, as the Patriots' nine conversions only faced an average third-down distance of 4.4 yards while the eight failures (not including a kneel-down) were tasked with an average distance of 10.1 yards. Four of those failed third downs were directly preceded by two penalties, one sack and one Ridley loss of 1 yard. The mistakes have put them in unconquerable spots.

"This game comes down to three phases," Edelman said. "That's the turnover ratio, third down and the red area, and we have to get better in two of those categories."

It was barely good enough to beat the Raiders. A testy Brady knew the offense couldn't skate by like that against future foes.

"It's good to be 2-1," Brady said. "But obviously there is a lot of room for improvement."■

Patriots defensive tackle Vince Wilfork celebrates with his teammates after coming up with the interception in the fourth quarter.

Inset: Wilfork celebrates after the game.

By Nancy Lane / Boston Herald

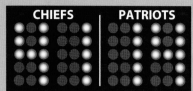

TOTAL BREAKDOWN

Pats appear lost on both sides of ball

By JEFF HOWE | *Boston Herald*

These weren't the Patriots of Tom Brady's and Bill Belichick's march to perennial title-questing dominance. But this version could become all too recognizable if widespread corrections aren't instituted in short order.

The Chiefs delivered a humbling blow of epic proportions last night, dropping the Pats, 41-14, at Arrowhead Stadium. Twice this season, the Patriots (2-2) have been on the wrong side of decisive beatings, but last night's was the second-most lopsided defeat of Bill Belichick's 15-year tenure.

"This was probably the most embarrassing game I've been a part of," safety Devin McCourty said. "We lost on every aspect."

Brady came unraveled in the second half and finished the night 14-of-23 for 159 yards, one touchdown and his first two interceptions of the season before he was benched in the fourth quarter. While a wilting offensive line and some untimely drops didn't help the cause, Brady's two picks weren't anywhere near his intended targets, and his final throw was returned for a touchdown.

"There's no one that is going to dig us out of this hole," Brady said. "We have to look each other in the eye."

The line again was a major concern. Left tackle Nate Solder and right tackle Sebastian Vollmer both were benched for Marcus Cannon during separate stretches, and the overhauled unit included first-time starting rookies Bryan Stork at center and Cameron Fleming at right guard, where he never played until last week's practices.

Offensively, the Patriots' woes were encapsulated by their opening trio of possessions in the third quarter. Down 17-0 at halftime with a glimmer of hope they could orchestrate a comeback to mimic last season's miracles against the Broncos and Browns, the Patriots fired a blank with a three-and-out that was capped by Justin Houston's strip sack.

Their next series ended with Tamba Hali's strip sack — thanks to Solder's whiff — that was recovered by the Chiefs, and it ultimately turned into Jamaal Charles' third touchdown of the night and a 24-0 score.

"You've got to get better," Solder said. "That's what you take from that, absolutely everyone, especially starting with myself."

Two plays later, Brady badly missed his bid for Julian Edelman, whose route didn't line up with the throw, and Sean Smith had a fair catch for an interception. Suddenly, a Chiefs defense that was the only unit without a takeaway all season had two in back-to-back possessions, and they turned that into Cairo Santos' 31-yard field goal and a 27-0 advantage.

Patriots running back Shane Vereen can't get any room to run in the fourth quarter.
By Matt West / Boston Herald

Patriots running back Shane Vereen is wrapped up by Kansas City Chiefs free safety Husain Abdullah on a first-quarter run.
By Matt West / Boston Herald

"We've all got to do a better job," Belichick said.

Oddly enough, the Patriots dressed five running backs and only three true receivers for the first time this season, but they only ran eight times on their first 27 plays while falling behind by 24 points. And for the second straight week against a porous run defense, they opened the game with three consecutive passing plays and a three-and-out.

But by that point, the blowout was in full motion and the exclamation point arrived by way of a fourth-quarter pick-six by Husain Abdullah, who jumped Brady's throw to Brandon LaFell and returned it 39 yards for a 41-7 lead.

Brady took a seat and backup Jimmy Garoppolo, in his first NFL appearance, was 6-of-7 for 70 yards and a TD.

Defensively, it wasn't much better. The Chiefs rushed for 207 yards, and Alex Smith was a cool 20-of-26 for 248 yards and three

Patriots QB Tom Brady shows his frustration on the bench.
By Matt West / Boston Herald

touchdowns. Jamaal Charles (18 carries for 92 yards, three catches for 16 yards and three total touchdowns) and Knile Davis (16 carries for 107 yards) were the beneficiaries of the Pats' front-seven woes, which allowed for clean holes and large chunks of yards off the edge.

When linebacker Jerod Mayo was asked if they know who they are yet, he replied, "I don't think so. It's early in the season. It's all about consistency. Right now, we're not consistent at any stage on the defensive side of the ball. We have to put together multiple games. That's what it's all about, getting hot and working together as a group. It's not just one person, one side. It's all of us." ▪

Brady fumbles the ball in the third quarter as he is hit by Kansas City Chiefs outside linebacker Tamba Hali.

By Matt West / Boston Herald

GAME STATISTICS	New England	0	0	7	7	—	14
	Kansas City	7	10	10	14	—	41

FIRST QUARTER

KC TD 2:15 Jamaal Charles 2 Yd Run (Cairo Santos Kick)
Drive: 11 plays, 73 yds, 5:58

SECOND QUARTER

KC TD 10:58 Jamaal Charles 5 Yd pass from Alex Smith (Cairo Santos Kick)
Drive: 3 plays, 86 yds, 1:27

KC FG 0:00 Cairo Santos 22 Yd Field Goal
Drive: 7 plays, 85 yds, 2:24

THIRD QUARTER

KC TD 7:53 Jamaal Charles 8 Yd pass from Alex Smith (Cairo Santos Kick)
Drive: 2 plays, 9 yds, 0:45

KC FG 5:29 Cairo Santos 31 Yd Field Goal
Drive: 4 plays, 0 yds, 1:34

NE TD 3:26 Brandon LaFell 44 Yd pass from Tom Brady (Stephen Gostkowski Kick)
Drive: 4 plays, 81 yds, 2:03

FOURTH QUARTER

KC TD 11:52 Travis Kelce 2 Yd pass from Alex Smith (Cairo Santos Kick)
Drive: 12 plays, 80 yds, 6:34

KC TD 10:34 Husain Abdullah 39 Yd Interception Return (Cairo Santos Kick)
Drive: 3 plays, 6 yds, 1:18

NE TD 7:25 Rob Gronkowski 13 Yd pass from Jimmy Garoppolo (Stephen Gostkowski Kick)
Drive: 7 plays, 81 yds, 3:09

TOM BRADY

Patriots quarterback Tom Brady meets up with Indianapolis Colts quarterback Andrew Luck at the end of the AFC Championship game.

By Matt Stone / Boston Herald

GUNSLINGER LOVES A SHOWDOWN

Brady gets better when the stakes are higher

By RON BORGES | *Boston Herald*

Perhaps Andrew Luck and all those who have wanted to rush him to the top of the NFL quarterbacking ladder learned a lesson in soggy Gillette Stadium last night. You can't be the Young Gun if you never pull your weapon.

For the fourth time in three years, young Luck came face-to-face with the fastest gun in football, and for the fourth time he left riddled with holes. Along with him this time went his upstart Colts teammates, who a week ago sent an Old

Gun, Peyton Manning, off to an uncertain future instead of back to an AFC Championship game showdown with his — and now Luck's — nemesis, Tom Brady.

The fact is the Colts weren't as good as the Denver Broncos, but Luck was faster on the draw than Manning, who was never able to pull the trigger because his quad was aching, his arm was sore, his neck was stiff and his gun wasn't loaded.

That set up the perfect scenario for the NFL's

26 **New England Patriots:** *SUPER BOWL XLIX*

Brady celebrates the first touchdown in the first quarter of the AFC Championship game.
By Matt Stone / Boston Herald

most important people — the marketing department. If Luck could beat Brady to the draw last night in the rain and gloom, he would be the league's new poster boy. It would have what it craves most: A fresh face with which to sell T-shirts, hats, game jerseys and ad spots.

But to do it, Luck had to outduel Brady as he had Manning, and he never came close. He opened the game with two incompletions, and before he knew it he was down 7-0 after punt returner Joshua Cribbs took a punt off the face to give the ball back to Brady at the Colts' 26-yard line. Six plays later, the game was over.

Technically it wasn't, but by halftime it was 17-7, the seven coming only because Brady made a Luck-like decision and tried to squeeze a pass into Rob Gronkowski surrounded near the goal line and linebacker D'Qwell Jackson picked it off at the Colts' 1.

It was then that the Young Gun had his moment. He led his team on a meandering, 10-play, 93-yard scoring drive that included a perfectly thrown 36-yard completion to T.Y. Hilton on third-and-8 with Kyle Arrington in near-perfect coverage.

It is throws like that which convince outside observers that a Young Gun lurks at the end of the street, waiting for the old marshal with the star on his chest now hanging slightly askew to see if he can beat him to the draw.

Luck completed two more passes on that drive to tight end Coby Fleener, cutting the Patriots' lead to 14-7 and giving hope to those who are always searching for someone new to become the fastest gun in town.

Hope, like Luck and the Colts, did not last long.

Brady answered that score with a 15-play, 65-yard drive to a field goal that ended the half 17-7, and then scored the next four times he got his hands on the ball to make it 45-7 by the time he holstered his pistol and went for a drink.

There was still 5:45 to play, but the crowd at

Brady gets extra yards as he runs
the ball in the second quarter of
the AFC Championship game.
By Matt Stone / Boston Herald

Gillette began to thunder down "Brady, Brady, Brady." It poured down over Luck's slumped shoulders harder than the rain was pelting down, as Brady sat on his bench, slowly waving, the conquering hero once again.

Then he rose up, hollering "Let's go!" over and over as he slapped hands with his posse on the sidelines. Meanwhile across the field, the Young Gun stood alone, stunned by what had befallen him.

There are many ways to describe what happened to Andrew Luck last night, but the most descriptive is this: He made two more tackles than he threw touchdown passes.

Playing in his first conference title game, Luck finished the day with two interceptions and a passer rating of 23. Even Geno Smith would have been embarrassed.

Across the field, The Old Gun proved he wasn't yet carrying a pop gun. He finished his night with his rookie coat holder, Jimmy Garoppolo, coming in with just over two minutes to play, so the same crowd that had booed Brady in the first half a week ago now could cheer him once again.

"There's a lot of motivation for a lot of different reasons, and I've had a lot of belief in my teammates over the course of the entire year," Brady said. "You don't want to judge your team after three or four games into the season. It's important not to ride the roller coaster. We put ourselves in a good position getting into the playoffs, won two home games and now we're in the Super Bowl. It's pretty sweet."

Sweet because his team won and sweet because he'd completed 23-of-35 passes to Luck's 12-of-33. He'd thrown for 100 more yards than Luck and three more touchdowns. He'd put more points on the board (45) than any previous Patriots' team had ever done in a playoff game, and as a consequence was going to be the starting quarterback in a record sixth Super Bowl.

The Young Gun had come to Foxboro with a notion that, after three previous failures, this night would be different — only to learn there's no new sheriff in town yet. Maybe there is in Denver, but not here in Foxboro.

Here was the same one whose been putting holes in guys like Andrew Luck for 14 years, and so the NFL's latest Young Gun went back home

Brady exults with his teammates after running back LaGarrette Blount scored a touchdown in the third quarter.

By Matt Stone / Boston Herald

wet, cold, disheveled and unsure of exactly what had just happened.

"It seemed like they were more on the details and we weren't," Luck said. "I know my play wasn't up to par for where it needs to be to give you a chance to beat a quality, quality team like them.

"It's hard to find much good right now. I guess you could say we took another step, but we had our sights set higher and obviously we're not there."

No he's not. Tom Brady is there. Again. Or rather still.

He's going to the Super Bowl, and another Young Gun in a Colts uniform with a live arm but a baffled mind is going on vacation, carrying with him a lot of question marks and no answers. ∎

Patriots tackle Nate Solder catches a touchdown pass from quarterback Tom Brady in the third quarter of the AFC Championship game.

By Matt Stone / Boston Herald

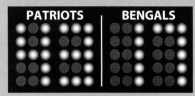

DO THE FIGHT THING

Feisty Pats are first to beat Cincy

By JEFF HOWE | *Boston Herald*

The Patriots came out of the locker room last night like a team that was sick of hearing how lousy it was all week.

For 60 minutes, the Pats fought both the Cincinnati Bengals and for themselves in an incredibly important gut-check performance, and they handed the NFL's last unbeaten team a 43-17 defeat. The Patriots spent the week vouching for their character and pride after an embarrassing loss to Kansas City, and they routinely pronounced they'd have to prove it by translating their message into actions. They made their point. "We knew what we showed (against the Chiefs) wasn't who we were," defensive tackle Vince Wilfork said. "The only way to do it is to do something about it, so we came out, executed well, said we were going to play well. That's what we did. You can call it angry. You can call it aggressive. Call it whatever you want to call it. We just said we have to play well, and we did."

The offensive explosion started right away, as they finally avoided a three-and-out to open the game for the first time this season and swiftly knifed through a Bengals defense that kept them out of the end zone during last year's meeting in Cincinnati.

Quarterback Tom Brady (23-of-35, 292 yards, two touchdowns) ain't dead yet and fired a 20-yard statement to wide receiver Brandon LaFell on the first play of the game, and running back Stevan Ridley capped the series with a 1-yard touchdown plunge that gave them a 7-0 lead.

Tight end Rob Gronkowski said the Patriots were sick of the criticism of Brady, and they wanted to deliver for him.

"I told my brother before we came to the game, ' I'm going to make 12 look like Tom Brady,' " Gronkowski

Patriots cornerback Kyle Arrington flips into the end zone with a third-quarter touchdown on a recovered fumble against the Cincinnati Bengals.

By Matt West / Boston Herald

Patriots running back Shane Vereen finds a hole thanks to tight end Rob Gronkowski.
By Nancy Lane / Boston Herald

said, with his voice filling with emotion. "And I went out there with my teammates, and we made Tom Brady look like Tom Brady after you guys were criticizing him all week — the fans, everything. And it feels so good."

The Pats showed some nastiness, too. Ridley and left tackle Nate Solder got into it with defensive lineman Wallace Gilberry on the opening series, and Gronkowski, Wilfork, defensive lineman Dominique Easley and running back Brandon Bolden also started skirmishes after the whistle in the opening half. The energy sometimes led to penalties, including four personal fouls before the break, but the angry passion was also a conduit to their success.

The Pats continued the hot start on the second series. Brady and Gronk hooked up for a 27-yard gain that pushed the QB past 50,000 career passing yards. Brady delivered a 17-yard touchdown strike to tight end Tim Wright for the 14-0 lead.

The defense was aided by cornerback Darrelle

Revis, who stood over the ball out of the huddle and marked Cincinnati's star receiver A.J. Green on every play, with the exception of Revis' second-half stint in the locker room for a hamstring injury. Andy Dalton was 3-of-5 for 63 yards when targeting a Revis-covered Green, but Revis also forced the wideout to fumble after an 18-yard gain in the second quarter, which led to kicker Stephen Gostkowski's 19-yard field goal that gave the Pats a 20-3 lead at the half.

"You can see the intensity that we had as the offense went out first," Revis said. "We kind of handled that on the defensive side as well."

And the Bengals, who averaged more carries per game than any team in the league, couldn't get going against a Pats rush defense that surrendered 398 yards in its two losses. Running backs Giovani Bernard and Jeremy Hill combined for 63 yards on 15 carries.

Meanwhile, Ridley gave the Pats a dimension they almost refused to acknowledge through much of their opening month. He had 27 carries for 113

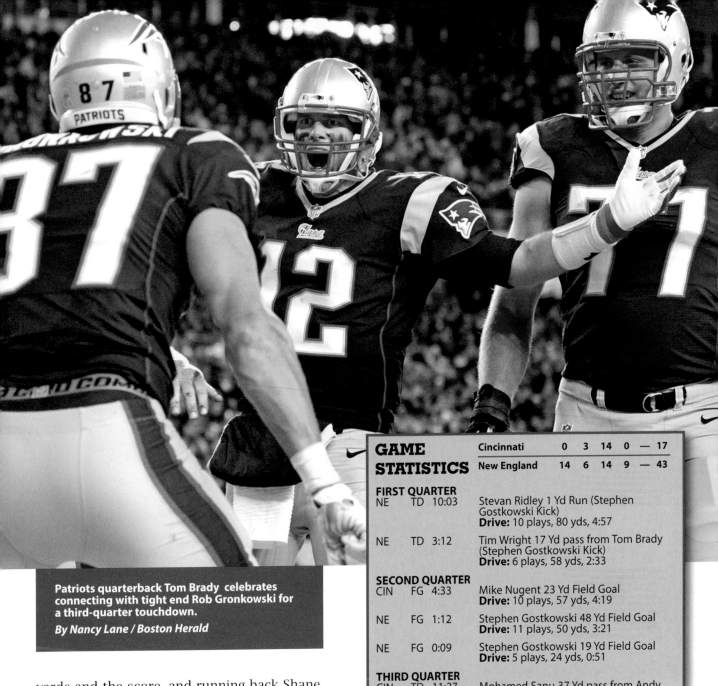

Patriots quarterback Tom Brady celebrates connecting with tight end Rob Gronkowski for a third-quarter touchdown.

By Nancy Lane / Boston Herald

GAME STATISTICS

Cincinnati	0	3	14	0	—	17
New England	14	6	14	9	—	43

FIRST QUARTER

NE TD 10:03 Stevan Ridley 1 Yd Run (Stephen Gostkowski Kick)
Drive: 10 plays, 80 yds, 4:57

NE TD 3:12 Tim Wright 17 Yd pass from Tom Brady (Stephen Gostkowski Kick)
Drive: 6 plays, 58 yds, 2:33

SECOND QUARTER

CIN FG 4:33 Mike Nugent 23 Yd Field Goal
Drive: 10 plays, 57 yds, 4:19

NE FG 1:12 Stephen Gostkowski 48 Yd Field Goal
Drive: 11 plays, 50 yds, 3:21

NE FG 0:09 Stephen Gostkowski 19 Yd Field Goal
Drive: 5 plays, 24 yds, 0:51

THIRD QUARTER

CIN TD 11:27 Mohamed Sanu 37 Yd pass from Andy Dalton (Mike Nugent Kick)
Drive: 1 plays, 37 yds, 0:05

NE TD 6:06 Rob Gronkowski 16 Yd pass from Tom Brady (Stephen Gostkowski Kick)
Drive: 10 plays, 86 yds, 5:21

NE TD 6:00 Kyle Arrington 9 Yd Fumble Return (Stephen Gostkowski Kick)
Drive: 0 plays, 0 yds, 0:06

CIN TD 3:43 A.J. Green 17 Yd pass from Andy Dalton (Mike Nugent Kick)
Drive: 6 plays, 82 yds, 2:17

FOURTH QUARTER

NE FG 14:54 Stephen Gostkowski 23 Yd Field Goal
Drive: 9 plays, 75 yds, 3:49

NE FG 7:53 Stephen Gostkowski 47 Yd Field Goal
Drive: 9 plays, 43 yds, 4:21

NE FG 2:55 Stephen Gostkowski 35 Yd Field Goal
Drive: 8 plays, 32 yds, 4:11

yards and the score, and running back Shane Vereen contributed nine carries for 90 yards.

The Pats were responsive, too. Dalton (15-of-24, 204 yards, two touchdowns) hit receiver Mohamed Sanu for a 37-yard TD to make it 20-10 in the third quarter, but Brady orchestrated a 10-play, 86-yard scoring drive right away.

Bolden then forced Brandon Tate to fumble the ensuing kickoff, and Kyle Arrington returned it 9 yards for the TD and a 34-10 lead.

Dalton hit Green for a 17-yard score to make it 34-17 on the next series, as Green beat cornerback Logan Ryan on the first play Revis missed, but that was as close as it got.

And now, the Patriots are on to Buffalo.∎

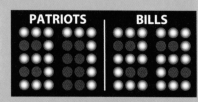

TOP OF THE HEAP

Injuries fail to derail Pats' climb to 1st place in AFC East

By JEFF HOWE | *Boston Herald*

If they were still standing, they were still fighting. The Patriots orchestrated a painfully resilient performance yesterday with a 37-22 win against the Buffalo Bills at Ralph Wilson Stadium to claim sole possession of the AFC East lead for the first time this season. Based on the way they've responded from an embarrassing defeat against the Chiefs, the Pats (4-2) know they've got the grit to overcome a host of challenges laid before them.

Tom Brady shook off an ankle injury to dismantle a Bills defense that had been teeing off on a replacement group of offensive linemen, and the quarterback completed 27-of-37 passes for 361 yards and four touchdowns. He did most of his work in the second half by hitting 15-of-17 passes for 274 yards and three touchdowns to keep his shorthanded team in control against the pesky Bills.

"We were aggressive, I think, all day," Brady said. "It was awesome. It was fun to be out there. Great team win. A lot of guys made a lot of big plays, so that's what we're going to need going forward. "Guys played their butts off." They did it for themselves, as a group that has refocused after a humbling defeat on Monday Night Football to win twice against teams that entered the game at least tied for first place in their respective divisions. But they also did it for fallen comrades, such as linebacker Jerod Mayo (knee), running back Stevan Ridley (knee) and offensive line captain Dan Connolly (concussion), who were all downed by serious injuries.

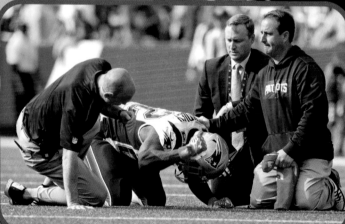

Patriots head coach Bill Belichick looks on as medical staff tend to injured middle linebacker Jerod Mayo in the second quarter.

Left Inset: Running back Stevan Ridley pounds the turf after getting injured in the third quarter.

Right Inset: Defensive tackle Vince Wilfork embraces injured Mayo as he is carted off.

By Nancy Lane / Boston Herald

Patriots wide receiver Julian Edelman is hauled down by Buffalo Bills cornerback Corey Graham in the second quarter.
By Nancy Lane / Boston Herald

"We feel like great teams in times like this, we've got to come out and play great ball," cornerback Darrelle Revis, who held Bills receiver Sammy Watkins to two catches for 27 yards, said. "We've done that the past two weeks." The Patriots needed a little bit from everybody in the first half. Linebacker Jamie Collins intercepted Kyle Orton's second-quarter pass to help the Pats get on the board, as Brady connected with tight end Tim Wright for a 1-yard touchdown and 7-0 lead.

After Mayo went down and the Bills tied it with Orton's 7-yard strike to Robert Woods,

defensive end Chandler Jones strip-sacked Orton, and Stephen Gostkowski nailed a 42-yard field goal. Safety Devin McCourty punched another ball free in the final seconds of the first half, and defensive end Zach Moore recovered Bills running back C.J. Spiller's fumble. Gostkowski's buzzer-beating 53-yard field goal made it 13-7 at the break.

But the Patriots were still teetering up front. Connolly went down, left tackle Nate Solder allowed a pair of sacks and right tackle Sebastian Vollmer surrendered one. Brady maintained his resolve to open the second half, firing a 17-yard pass to receiver Brandon LaFell (four catches, 97 yards, two touchdowns) on third-and-9 and then lofting a 43-yard pass that culminated with wideout Brian Tyms' acrobatic touchdown reception that made it 20-7.

"I always try to attack the ball," said Tyms of his first catch of a Brady pass. "I just wanted the ball. I wanted the ball more. I'm not going to run 40 yards without the ball."

The Bills kept the pressure on when back Fred Jackson's 1-yard touchdown plunge cut it to 20-14 and Gostkowski's 40-yard field goal extended the margin to 23-14. Orton got the Bills to the Pats 21, but a penalty and one of defensive end Rob Ninkovich's three sacks halted their march.

And after tight end Rob Gronkowski (seven receptions, 94 yards) had a touchdown nullified by guard Jordan Devey's holding penalty, Brady found a streaking LaFell for an 18-yard score on third-and-12 to make it 30-14. The Pats converted 7-of-15 third downs — 4-of-5 in the second half.

When the Bills refused to go away yet again in new owner Terry Pegula's first game, Brady put his foot on their throat a final time. Orton (24-of-38, 299 yards, two touchdowns, interception) connected with Chris Hogan for an 8-yard touchdown before his two-point conversion toss to Woods cut it to 30-22. Brady, backed up on his own 6-yard line, dug the Pats out for the umpteenth time. He found Gronkowski for 17 yards on third-and-16, and two plays later, Brady delivered a perfect pass when LaFell got behind the defense for a 56-yard touchdown.

"Any way we can get a touchdown to put this game out of reach," LaFell said, "you have to get it."

Through humiliation, soul-searching accountability checks and injuries, the Patriots have revealed their resiliency.

"We're sticking together, and guys are really playing for each other," Revis said. ∎

GAME STATISTICS

			New England	0	13	10	14	—	37
			Buffalo	0	7	7	8	—	22

SECOND QUARTER

NE TD 13:04 Tim Wright 1 Yd pass from Tom Brady (Stephen Gostkowski Kick)
Drive: 5 plays, 61 yds, 1:49

BUF TD 3:52 Robert Woods 7 Yd pass from Kyle Orton (Dan Carpenter Kick)
Drive: 10 plays, 67 yds, 4:51

NE FG 1:43 Stephen Gostkowski 42 Yd Field Goal
Drive: 4 plays, 0 yds, 0:26

NE FG 0:00 Stephen Gostkowski 53 Yd Field Goal
Drive: 2 plays, 7 yds, 0:06

THIRD QUARTER

NE TD 12:30 Brian Tyms 43 Yd pass from Tom Brady (Stephen Gostkowski Kick)
Drive: 6 plays, 80 yds, 2:30

BUF TD 5:33 Fred Jackson 1 Yd Run (Dan Carpenter Kick)
Drive: 13 plays, 80 yds, 6:57

NE FG 3:08 Stephen Gostkowski 40 Yd Field Goal
Drive: 6 plays, 56 yds, 2:25

FOURTH QUARTER

NE TD 8:42 Brandon LaFell 18 Yd pass from Tom Brady (Stephen Gostkowski Kick)
Drive: 12 plays, 80 yds, 6:08

BUF TD 5:58 Chris Hogan 8 Yd pass from Kyle Orton (Kyle Orton Pass to Robert Woods for Two-Point Conversion)
Drive: 8 plays, 80 yds, 2:44

NE TD 2:49 Brandon LaFell 56 Yd pass from Tom Brady (Stephen Gostkowski Kick)
Drive: 7 plays, 93 yds, 3:09

Patriots defensive end Rob Ninkovich sacks Buffalo Bills quarterback Kyle Orton in the second quarter.
By Nancy Lane / Boston Herald

Patriots tight end Rob Gronkowski's fourth-quarter touchdown was nullified by an offensive holding penalty.
By Nancy Lane / Boston Herald

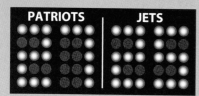

**REGULAR SEASON
> GAME 7**

Oct. 16, 2014

JETS @ PATRIOTS

PATS BLOCK, PARTY

Jones nixes rival's late FG attempt

By JEFF HOWE | *Boston Herald*

There was a hint of redemption in the air last night for the Patriots.

They outlasted the Jets, 27-25, at Gillette Stadium to improve to 5-2 and bury their rivals at the bottom of the division. With some extra time to prepare, the Patriots will get ready to host the Bears and Broncos before their bye week.

Patriots defensive tackle Chris Jones blocked Nick Folk's 58-yard bid for a game-winning field goal to secure the victory at the buzzer, which was a fitting conclusion to a rugged fight with the Jets. Last season, Jones was flagged for an illegal pushing penalty that led to Folk's overtime winner at MetLife Stadium.

"I thought it was so fitting that he made that play," Bill Belichick said. "That was awesome."

Folk made four field goals earlier in the game (22, 47, 46, 27), so the Patriots were well-versed with the Jets' operation. But the Patriots didn't save any secret play call for the final bid.

"They were pretty stout," Jones said. "I think it was just coming down to will at the end. We just had to see who could get the most push in the front, and we ended up getting it."

Earlier in the fourth quarter, Pats receiver Danny Amendola had his greatest moment in a tumultuous season. The $31 million free agent acquisition from the 2013 offseason caught a 19-yard touchdown pass from Tom Brady (20-of-37, 261 yards, three touchdowns) that gave the Pats a 27-19 lead with 7:49 remaining. Brady rolled to his left as Amendola broke off his route and shot up the left seam toward the end zone, where he made a spinning catch to extend a tight margin.

"Always have a point to prove," said Amendola, who has had more catches and yards called back by penalties

Patriots defensive end Rob Ninkovich celebrates defensive end Chandler Jones' sack on New York Jets quarterback Geno Smith during the fourth quarter.

By Matt Stone / Boston Herald

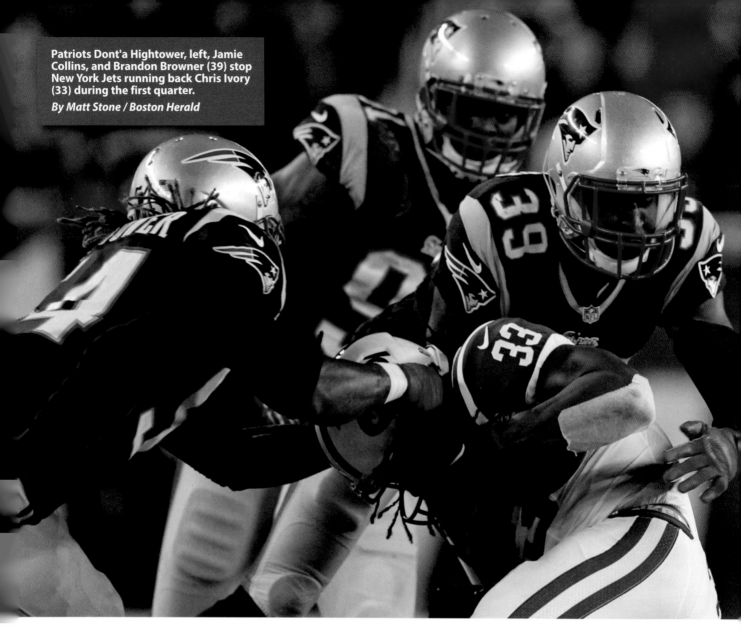

Patriots Dont'a Hightower, left, Jamie Collins, and Brandon Browner (39) stop New York Jets running back Chris Ivory (33) during the first quarter.

By Matt Stone / Boston Herald

(five for 71) than credited to his stat total this season (five for 42). "You have to play with a chip on your shoulder, and I bring that attitude into every single game."

Yet, the Jets wouldn't quit. Geno Smith (20-of-34, 226 yards, TD) orchestrated a 12-play, 86-yard touchdown drive that was capped with Jeff Cumberland's 10-yard catch on third-and-6, which was one of the Jets' nine third-down conversions on 16 tries. But the two-point conversion failed when Smith's fade pass for Jace Amaro sailed through the end zone.

Fittingly, Amendola recovered the ensuing onside kick, which he believed was the first time he has ever done that.

"It was a good night for our whole team," Amendola said. "We came out with a win. I almost had a heart attack at the end, but the defense came up huge with a stop and the blocked field goal."

Even after the recovery, the Patriots were reaching for the Lipitor. They went three-and-out for the fourth time while trying to run out the clock, and Smith took over at his own 12 with 1:06 remaining but no timeouts. Somehow, an offense that had all the time in the world (40:54 in time of possession) managed to pick up the pace and march to the Pats 40 before Jones' block party.

"That's what rivalries are," said cornerback Darrelle Revis, who wouldn't bite on the significance of the game from a personal perspective. "It doesn't really matter what the record may be for any team. This is historically our rivals. It's been going on for years and years. It probably will continue to be a rivalry. You never know what you're going to get in these games, and they're always tough."

The Patriots came flying out of the locker room again, as Brady opened the game with a 49-yard touchdown pass to running back Shane Vereen (five receptions for 71 yards, 11 carries for 43 yards) for a 7-0 lead. Brady and Vereen connected for a 3-yard score in the second quarter to make it 14-9, but the Jets kept chipping away with Folk's field goals.

Jets running back Chris Ivory (21 carries, 107 yards) scored a 1-yard touchdown to give the Jets a 19-17 lead in the third quarter on their fifth consecutive scoring drive to open the game. But the Pats dug in from there.

"It just shows you the chemistry we've got and how in sync we are as a team, as a whole," Revis said. "We bond well. Everybody on this team bonds well. We don't put the finger at anybody, whether somebody makes a mental error in the game or a penalty. We lift each other up, and we go play the next play. Guys have been doing that all year long, and we're going to stay with that type of mentality as a team." ∎

The Patriots block a 58-yard field goal attempt by the New York Jets during the fourth quarter.

By Christopher Evans / Boston Herald

Inset Left: Quarterback Tom Brady, right, hugs wide receiver Danny Amendola after his touchdown pass during the fourth quarter.

By Matt Stone / Boston Herald

Inset Right: Amendola celebrates with fans after scoring a touchdown in the fourth quarter.

By Christopher Evans / Boston Herald

GAME STATISTICS

New York Jets	6	6	7	6	—	25
New England	7	10	3	7	—	27

FIRST QUARTER

NE   TD   13:31   Shane Vereen 49 Yd pass from Tom Brady (Stephen Gostkowski Kick)
Drive: 4 plays, 80 yds, 1:29

NYJ   FG   6:29   Nick Folk 22 Yd Field Goal
Drive: 12 plays, 76 yds, 7:02

NYJ   FG   0:19   Nick Folk 47 Yd Field Goal
Drive: 10 plays, 46 yds, 5:22

SECOND QUARTER

NYJ   FG   7:52   Nick Folk 46 Yd Field Goal
Drive: 12 plays, 32 yds, 6:18

NE   TD   4:22   Shane Vereen 3 Yd pass from Tom Brady (Stephen Gostkowski Kick)
Drive: 10 plays, 80 yds, 3:30

NYJ   FG   1:01   Nick Folk 27 Yd Field Goal
Drive: 9 plays, 32 yds, 3:21

NE   FG   0:00   Stephen Gostkowski 39 Yd Field Goal
Drive: 9 plays, 53 yds, 1:01

THIRD QUARTER

NYJ   TD   8:58   Chris Ivory 1 Yd Run (Nick Folk Kick)
Drive: 11 plays, 80 yds, 6:02

NE   FG   4:10   Stephen Gostkowski 36 Yd Field Goal
Drive: 10 plays, 53 yds, 4:48

FOURTH QUARTER

NE   TD   7:49   Danny Amendola 19 Yd pass from Tom Brady (Stephen Gostkowski Kick)
Drive: 7 plays, 46 yds, 3:02

NYJ   TD   2:31   Jeff Cumberland 10 Yd pass from Geno Smith (Two-Point Pass Conversion Failed)
Drive: 12 plays, 86 yds, 5:18

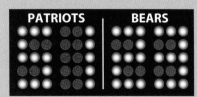

THE TOM-INATOR

Offense rips Bears apart with Peyton's Broncos on horizon

By JEFF HOWE | *Boston Herald*

The operation took a bit longer than expected, but the Patriots look like a machine again, just in time for the Denver Broncos to come to town. The Pats mauled the Chicago Bears, 51-23, at Gillette Stadium to win their fourth consecutive game, and they'll host the Broncos next Sunday with a chance to leapfrog the reigning AFC champions for the best record in the conference. While Peyton Manning continues to pile up records and the Broncos (6-1) claim the crown in the court of public opinion, the Patriots (6-2) served notice they're still pretty good, too.

"We know what's at stake," cornerback Darrelle Revis said. "We know Denver is a great team, and we've got a lot of respect. But at the same time, we're trying to accomplish something, as they are, too. It's the battle of the AFC. We understand. We totally understand. These are the games you want to play for. I can speak for everybody that is on this team. We live for games like this."

Tom Brady lit up the Bears' ragged defense by completing 30-of-35 passes for 354 yards and his fifth career five-touchdown game, and tight end Rob Gronkowski once again looked invincible, catching nine passes for 149 yards and three touchdowns, including a final score when he emasculated safety Ryan Mundy with a stiff-arm before finishing off a 46-yard catch and run. Wide receiver Brandon LaFell had the game of his life with 11 receptions for 124 yards and a score, giving him a three-game total of 19 catches for 276 yards and three trips to the end zone.

"There were a lot of big plays and we got a lot of momentum, so it was a fun day," said Brady, whose 85.7 completion percentage was the second-highest of his career. "Those don't happen like that very often."

Revis pitched his first shutout of the season to lead the defense. Bears quarterback Jay Cutler threw five incompletions, including an interception, when aiming for the Island. Cutler completed 20-of-30 passes for 227 yards, three touchdowns, one pick and piled up his stats in garbage time, which essentially began late in the second quarter.

The Patriots embarrassed the Bears right out of the chute, storming down the field in five plays for a touchdown on their first possession. Gronkowski capped the drive by catching a 6-yard fade over Mundy for a 7-0 lead.

Stephen Gostkowski's 23-yard field goal closed a more methodical 17-play drive on their second possession, but Brady made sure to finish the job on their third series by hitting tight end Tim Wright (seven receptions, 61 yards)

Patriots quarterback Tom Brady celebrates defensive end Rob Ninkovich's fumble recovery and touchdown during the first quarter.

By Matt Stone / Boston Herald

Patriots defensive tackle Dominique Easley sacks Chicago Bears quarterback Jay Cutler during the third quarter.

By Matt Stone / Boston Herald

for a 1-yard score and 17-0 advantage with 8:09 to play in the second quarter.

The Bears made a peep when Cutler found Matt Forte (168 yards from scrimmage) for a 25-yard touchdown that cut it to 17-7, but things got ugly after that. Brady and Gronkowski hooked up for an impressive, toe-tapping 2-yard touchdown to make it 24-7. After the Bears' quick three-and-out and Julian Edelman's 42-yard punt return, Brady orchestrated an efficient one-play touchdown drive by hitting LaFell for a 9-yard score and a 31-7 lead.

Defensive lineman Zach Moore and linebacker Dont'a Hightower teamed up to strip-sack Cutler on the next play, and defensive end Rob Ninkovich scooped up the fumble and returned it 15 yards for a touchdown and 38-7 advantage with 55 seconds to play in the first half. The Pats scored 21 of their 31 second-quarter points in 57 seconds, and it seemed like all that was missing was a butt fumble.

"Whenever we see those guys making plays,

we know if we just can keep getting them back out there, they'll keep scoring," safety Devin McCourty said. "And that's how you blow games open."

Brady and Gronkowski rubbed it in with the first drive in the third quarter. Gronkowski caught a pass by the left sideline, threw Mundy aside and scampered down the field for a 46-yard score that pushed the margin to 45-7. Gronkowski's damage was done three minutes into the third quarter and departed for the day due to dehydration.

"I've got to make sure I don't get dehydrated," Gronkowski said. "I've got to keep on drinking."

Dry mouth is about the only thing that could slow down the Pats as they hit their peak so far this season. They have outscored their last four opponents, 158-87, and they finally look like they're ready for Manning's visit.

"Last time we saw those guys, they handled us pretty good, so I think all the guys in this locker room that were there remember that," McCourty said. "We know what we need to do." ∎

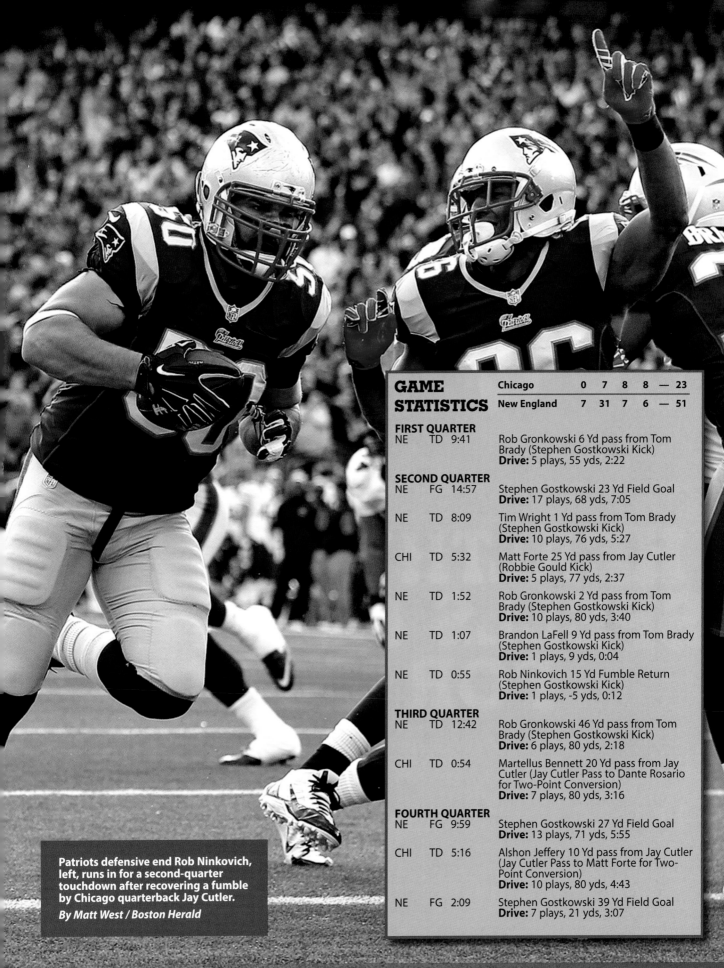

Patriots defensive end Rob Ninkovich, left, runs in for a second-quarter touchdown after recovering a fumble by Chicago quarterback Jay Cutler.

By Matt West / Boston Herald

GAME STATISTICS

	1	2	3	4		Final
Chicago	0	7	8	8	—	23
New England	7	31	7	6	—	51

FIRST QUARTER

NE   TD 9:41   Rob Gronkowski 6 Yd pass from Tom Brady (Stephen Gostkowski Kick)
Drive: 5 plays, 55 yds, 2:22

SECOND QUARTER

NE   FG 14:57   Stephen Gostkowski 23 Yd Field Goal
Drive: 17 plays, 68 yds, 7:05

NE   TD 8:09   Tim Wright 1 Yd pass from Tom Brady (Stephen Gostkowski Kick)
Drive: 10 plays, 76 yds, 5:27

CHI   TD 5:32   Matt Forte 25 Yd pass from Jay Cutler (Robbie Gould Kick)
Drive: 5 plays, 77 yds, 2:37

NE   TD 1:52   Rob Gronkowski 2 Yd pass from Tom Brady (Stephen Gostkowski Kick)
Drive: 10 plays, 80 yds, 3:40

NE   TD 1:07   Brandon LaFell 9 Yd pass from Tom Brady (Stephen Gostkowski Kick)
Drive: 1 plays, 9 yds, 0:04

NE   TD 0:55   Rob Ninkovich 15 Yd Fumble Return (Stephen Gostkowski Kick)
Drive: 1 plays, -5 yds, 0:12

THIRD QUARTER

NE   TD 12:42   Rob Gronkowski 46 Yd pass from Tom Brady (Stephen Gostkowski Kick)
Drive: 6 plays, 80 yds, 2:18

CHI   TD 0:54   Martellus Bennett 20 Yd pass from Jay Cutler (Jay Cutler Pass to Dante Rosario for Two-Point Conversion)
Drive: 7 plays, 80 yds, 3:16

FOURTH QUARTER

NE   FG 9:59   Stephen Gostkowski 27 Yd Field Goal
Drive: 13 plays, 71 yds, 5:55

CHI   TD 5:16   Alshon Jeffery 10 Yd pass from Jay Cutler (Jay Cutler Pass to Matt Forte for Two-Point Conversion)
Drive: 10 plays, 80 yds, 4:43

NE   FG 2:09   Stephen Gostkowski 39 Yd Field Goal
Drive: 7 plays, 21 yds, 3:07

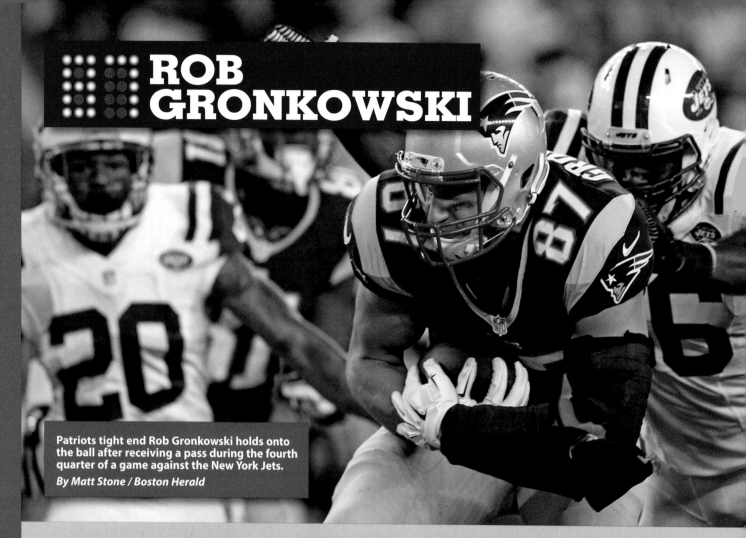

ROB GRONKOWSKI

Patriots tight end Rob Gronkowski holds onto the ball after receiving a pass during the fourth quarter of a game against the New York Jets.

By Matt Stone / Boston Herald

HEALTHY GRONK SPELLS DISASTER FOR FOES

Unstoppable force just what the doctor ordered

By KAREN GUREGIAN | *Boston Herald*

During the past two postseasons, the Patriots couldn't get over the hump while Rob Gronkowski, one of the most devastating offensive weapons in the league, watched as a helpless spectator.

They fell short of competing for the Super Bowl, as the most feared tight end in the business was bouncing from one operating room to another.

Going Gronk-less is like going to the prom without a date. There's no spark, and no fun.

But tomorrow, things are different. Gronkowski is healthy after making it through his comeback season from surgery to repair a torn ACL, a comeback that defied most medical odds.

As difference-makers go, there might not be one any more significant than Gronkowski in these playoffs.

Gronkowski's typical celebration of a touchdown in a game against the Buffalo Bills.

By Nancy Lane / Boston Herald

And he's chomping at the bit. Tomorrow can't come fast enough for the all-world, All-Pro tight end.

"I'm super-excited. I'm super-pumped," Gronkowski said in a quiet moment at his locker while preparing for the divisional round showdown with the Baltimore Ravens. "I'll probably have some jitters, the closer we get. It's been a while. But I can't wait. I'll be ready to go." Will he ever. Many of his teammates know that deep, dark place Gronk is coming from because they've watched him work so hard to get to this stage. They remember the litany of injuries, and seeing him carted off the field with that dreaded ACL/ MCL tear in December 2013.

They've watched him work through all the rehabs, and finally, get through a season unscathed to reach this point. They know how hungry he is to suit up and play in the one-and-done games, the ones that lead to the Super Bowl.

"He'll be ready. I know that," said fellow tight end Michael Hoomanawanui. "After such a gruesome injury, it'll be great to see him out there. He's such a big part of the team.

"It's a testament to his will and his dedication," Hoomanawanui added. "I've said it from Day 1 since I've been around him, you can see it. He's in here early, stays late. He's dedicated to the team, and puts the team first. That's the kind of person he is. And, that's what we're going to need going forward."

Gronkowski, whose 1,124 yards and 12 touchdowns led all NFL tight ends this season, has had his game face on all week. Even members of his family, many of whom will be on hand at Gillette for the game, know the significance of the moment, and are thankful he's made it back this far after a trying few years spent rehabbing a virtual buffet of injuries.

They know about the doubts that crept in, especially after he blew out his knee and feared he might not be the same, or ever play again.

"We are so glad Rob has made it through the season and into the playoffs and is feeling great!" his mother, Diane, said. "He's worked extremely hard, physically and mentally, for a long time, to get back to where he is. He is very dedicated to his team, and wants to be out there working with his teammates."

After ankle, multiple forearm, back and knee surgeries that all took place over the course of the last three years, Gronk is back to being Gronk again.

Ravens coach John Harbaugh knows what that means, and what's in store. He knows the beast has been unleashed, and

Gronkowski celebrates his a touchdown with fullback James Develin.

By Nancy Lane / Boston Herald

what he's bound to see in tomorrow's game.

"He's one of the best. He's big; he's fast; he's tough; he's nasty," Harbaugh said during a press conference earlier in the week. "He gets the ball in his hands and he wants to punish people — after the catch, he's trying to run everybody he can over. He's just a gifted guy, and they get him the ball, and they get him the ball quickly, and they give him the ball downfield."

NFL Network analyst and former Patriots fullback Heath Evans isn't quite sure how Harbaugh is going to tame Gronk. In fact, asked Wednesday on NFL Network who the Seahawks' biggest threat to possible back-to-back titles was, Evans said it wasn't a team that came to mind, but Gronkowski.

"He's the one guy that when Tom (Brady) is protected for two and a half, three seconds consistently, no one has ever had an answer for him," Evans said when reached last night. "When he's healthy … which he is, no one's had an answer for him.

"I'm sorry to sound so cliche, but Rob is a matchup nightmare. He's a double-team mismatch," Evans added. "Safeties are too small and linebackers are too slow. Those things are true, but it really doesn't quantify the issues that he creates. His ball skills are second to none, and I'm putting him up there with wide receivers. It's absolutely crazy what he can do. And I know (Ravens defensive coordinator) Dean Pees is losing sleep over what the possibilities are for Rob."

Evans said the Ravens' one hope is if they are able to bring middle pressure on Brady with Haloti Ngata and Chris Canty, where the Patriots quarterback can't manipulate the pocket and make plays. If they aren't able to do that, lights out.

"One way or another, if protection is even so-so, Rob will have a huge impact on the game," said Evans. "Even if you commit extra resources and take Rob off the stat sheet, with Brandon LaFell and Julian Edelman, it's the trickle-down effect, they'll just beat you elsewhere.

"But I just love the kid," he went on. "He's such a football-junkie meathead, and I don't mean that to be a knock. I think that's a great thing. This guy's life revolves around this. That's why Bill puts up with the spiking of the football and all that. He knows at the core, this is a guy who loves football and wants what's best for the team."

What's best for the team is having a healthy Gronk right here, right now, playing when it matters most. We're on the eve of the Pats' first playoff game, and No. 87 is all revved up and ready to go.

"I'll be amped up and ready," said Gronk, "but you don't want to go too overboard. You still have to be focused and prepared. It's the playoffs. It's a one-game season. You want to play to the max of your ability."

If Gronk hits that max, the Patriots will surely get over the hump. ∎

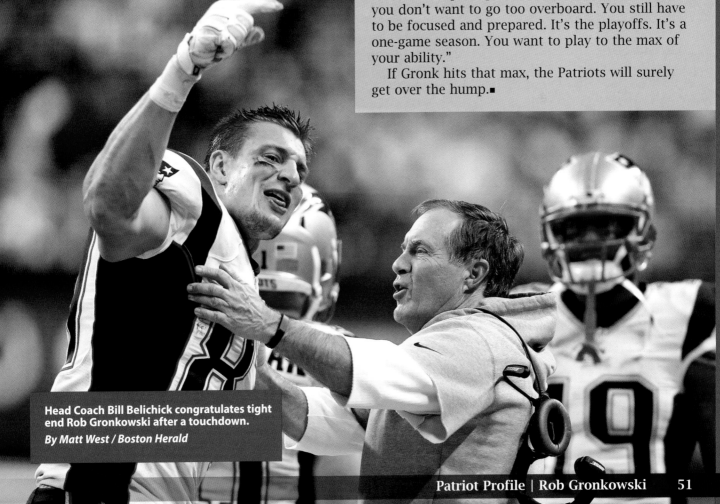

Head Coach Bill Belichick congratulates tight end Rob Gronkowski after a touchdown.
By Matt West / Boston Herald

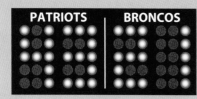

BACK IN THE SADDLE

Pats buck Broncs to corral AFC

By JEFF HOWE | *Boston Herald*

The AFC now runs through New England. The Patriots blasted the Denver Broncos, 43-21, at Gillette Stadium to improve to 7-2 and grab the top seed in the conference, while the 6-2 Broncos lost for the first time since a Week 3 Super Bowl rematch against the Seattle Seahawks.

Tom Brady was superior to Peyton Manning in every way, claiming his 11th victory in the 16th edition of the rivalry between the pair of future Hall of Famers. Brady completed 33-of-53 passes for 333 yards, four touchdowns and one interception, and his lesser-acclaimed targets were the more vaunted catalysts.

"He is playing unbelievable right now," tight end Rob Gronkowski said.

Gronkowski again led the way with nine receptions for 105 yards and a score while wide receivers Julian Edelman and Brandon LaFell and running back Shane Vereen helped Brady spread the wealth.

"When (Brady) is on like he did today, I don't think there's anybody better," LaFell said. "When our offense is flowing, everybody getting the ball, we're really tough to stop."

Manning was 34-of-57 for 438 yards, two touchdowns and two interceptions, but he racked up yards when the game was out of reach. His two mistakes led to a pair of Pats touchdowns that spawned a first-half rally and aided the second-half whooping that culminated with the Patriots claiming early control of the conference.

"It's very important because we want home-field advantage," cornerback Darrelle Revis said. "We definitely do. I think that's one of our goals, but we've got to take it one week at a time. This week, it was Denver. People might say this is the battle of the AFC, and that's fine. It's two great teams playing."

The Patriots Akeem Ayers celebrates
sacking Denver Broncos quarterback
Peyton Manning in the second quarter.
By Nancy Lane / Boston Herald

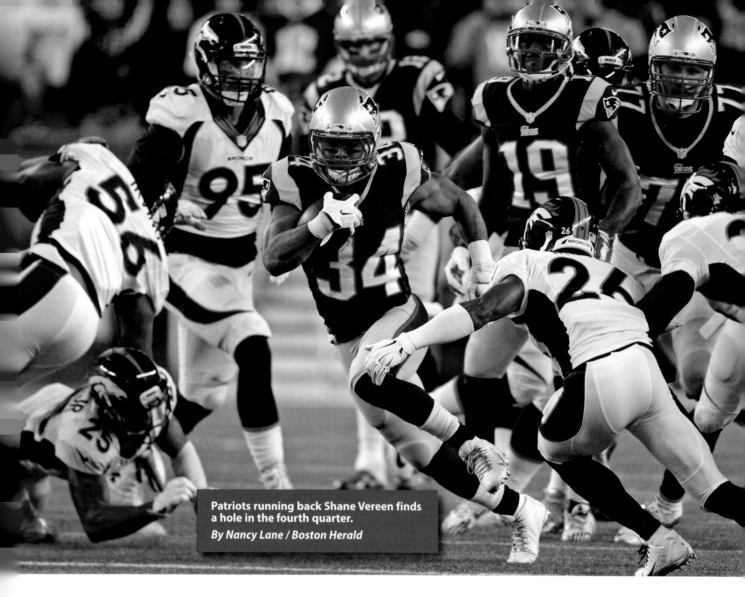

Patriots running back Shane Vereen finds a hole in the fourth quarter.
By Nancy Lane / Boston Herald

The Patriots held the Broncos in check despite a mini-rally in the second half. Tight end Julius Thomas, who wasn't targeted in the first half, caught an 18-yard touchdown pass to trim the margin to 27-14 with 11:06 left in the third quarter. The Pats responded by converting once on third and fourth downs on the following drive to set up Stephen Gostkowski's 45-yard field goal into the wind for a 30-14 lead.

Manning targeted Wes Welker on the next play, but cornerback Brandon Browner intercepted the deflected pass and returned it 30 yards to the Broncos 10. Brady immediately found LaFell, who overcame three earlier drops, to put the nail in the coffin at 37-14.

Manning and Ronnie Hillman hooked up for a 15-yard score, but the Broncos' rebuilt defense once again folded. The Pats, who converted 6-of-16 third downs in the game, had two on a drive that culminated with Gronkowski's 1-yard touchdown catch past Von Miller, which gave the hosts a 43-21 lead early in the fourth quarter. The Pats held the Broncos scoreless in their final

four possessions.

The Patriots held the Broncos to back-to-back three-and-outs to open the game, and Gostkowski's 49-yard field goal gave them a lead midway through the first quarter.

Manning, though, responded by attacking the heart of the Pats' defense, completing three passes against Revis for 56 yards on the ensuing drive, and Browner was flagged for pass interference in the end zone before Hillman's 1-yard touchdown made it 7-3.

Gostkowski's 29-yard chip shot cut the deficit to 7-6 early in the second quarter, and defensive end Rob Ninkovich kicked things into gear two plays later. Ninkovich dropped into a zone in front of Demaryius Thomas (seven receptions for 127 yards) and an unsuspecting Manning, who threw his first interception of the game. The Patriots finally found the end zone, as Brady connected with Edelman for a 5-yard score and 13-7 advantage with 11:41 remaining in the second. Edelman beat T.J. Ward, who riled up the Pats earlier with a low shot on Gronkowski's knees, to

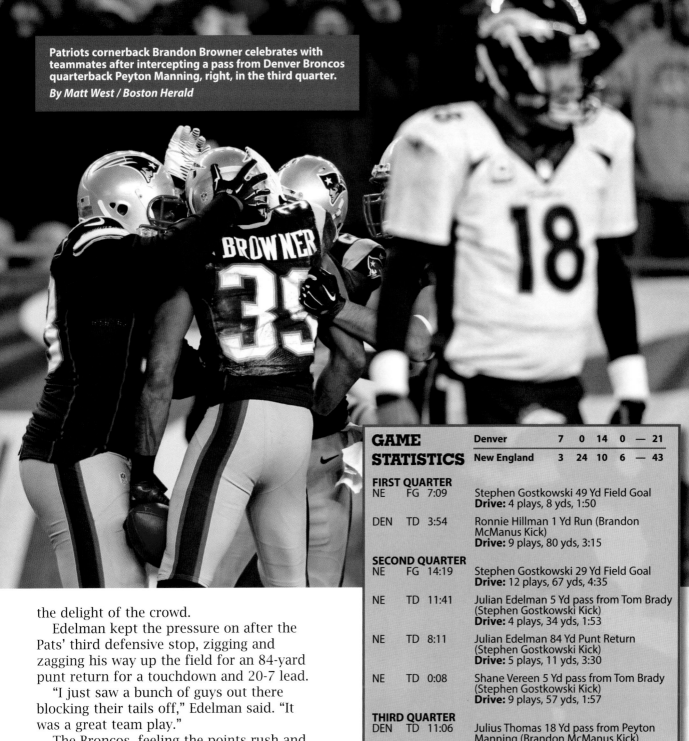

Patriots cornerback Brandon Browner celebrates with teammates after intercepting a pass from Denver Broncos quarterback Peyton Manning, right, in the third quarter.

By Matt West / Boston Herald

GAME STATISTICS		Denver	7	0	14	0	—	21
		New England	3	24	10	6	—	43

FIRST QUARTER

NE — FG — 7:09 — Stephen Gostkowski 49 Yd Field Goal
Drive: 4 plays, 8 yds, 1:50

DEN — TD — 3:54 — Ronnie Hillman 1 Yd Run (Brandon McManus Kick)
Drive: 9 plays, 80 yds, 3:15

SECOND QUARTER

NE — FG — 14:19 — Stephen Gostkowski 29 Yd Field Goal
Drive: 12 plays, 67 yds, 4:35

NE — TD — 11:41 — Julian Edelman 5 Yd pass from Tom Brady (Stephen Gostkowski Kick)
Drive: 4 plays, 34 yds, 1:53

NE — TD — 8:11 — Julian Edelman 84 Yd Punt Return (Stephen Gostkowski Kick)
Drive: 5 plays, 11 yds, 3:30

NE — TD — 0:08 — Shane Vereen 5 Yd pass from Tom Brady (Stephen Gostkowski Kick)
Drive: 9 plays, 57 yds, 1:57

THIRD QUARTER

DEN — TD — 11:06 — Julius Thomas 18 Yd pass from Peyton Manning (Brandon McManus Kick)
Drive: 6 plays, 57 yds, 2:24

NE — FG — 7:46 — Stephen Gostkowski 45 Yd Field Goal
Drive: 12 plays, 53 yds, 3:20

NE — TD — 7:27 — Brandon LaFell 10 Yd pass from Tom Brady (Stephen Gostkowski Kick)
Drive: 1 plays, 10 yds, 0:04

DEN — TD — 5:50 — Ronnie Hillman 15 Yd pass from Peyton Manning (Brandon McManus Kick)
Drive: 4 plays, 72 yds, 1:37

FOURTH QUARTER

NE — TD — 13:57 — Rob Gronkowski 1 Yd pass from Tom Brady (Pass Failed)
Drive: 14 plays, 80 yds, 6:53

the delight of the crowd.

Edelman kept the pressure on after the Pats' third defensive stop, zigging and zagging his way up the field for an 84-yard punt return for a touchdown and 20-7 lead.

"I just saw a bunch of guys out there blocking their tails off," Edelman said. "It was a great team play."

The Broncos, feeling the points rush and employing a kicker who already missed a 41-yard try, went for it on fourth-and-6 from the Pats 34, and linebacker Akeem Ayers recorded his second sack in as many games by taking down Manning with 2:05 left in the half.

Brady hit Edelman with a 26-yard strike and, later in the drive, his 5-yard touchdown pass to Edelman was overturned on review, but the quarterback found Vereen from the same distance for a 27-7 lead with 8 seconds left in the half. ∎

On the play of the game, New England Patriots cornerback Brandon Browner, right, picks off a pass intended for Denver Broncos wide receiver Wes Welker in the third quarter.

By Matt West / Boston Herald

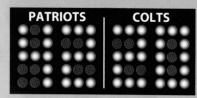

PATS IN COMMAND

Ride rout of Colts to top of AFC

By JEFF HOWE | *Boston Herald*

Even with Tom Brady not performing like Tom Brady, the Patriots still dismantled another battle-tested opponent. The Pats crushed the Colts, 42-20, at Lucas Oil Stadium to improve to 8-2 and take sole possession of the best record in the AFC. They were the conference's lone division leader to win in Week 11.

Brady completed 19-of-30 passes for 257 yards, two touchdowns and a pair of egregious first-half interceptions, but running back Jonas Gray had his back with career highs of 37 carries, 201 yards and four touchdowns. The defense held the NFL's top-rated offense to its fewest points of the season, and cornerback Darrelle Revis was a major force once again.

Colts quarterback Andrew Luck was 1-of-6 for 5 yards and an interception when targeting Revis, and the only completion was a failed third down.

"Even though we would love it for Tom to throw seven touchdowns in a game, sometimes it might not be like that," Revis said. "Sometimes, the defense has to lift the offense up. Sometimes, special teams has to lift the defense and offense up. As long as we just continue to play consistent, we'll be fine."

Luck was 23-of-39 for 303 yards, two touchdowns and the pick, but he joined Peyton Manning as Patriots adversaries who posted nice stats in relatively meaningless fashion.

"I think we do a good job of understanding there's a certain way to play these great quarterbacks," said safety Devin McCourty, who intercepted Revis' tipped pass in the second quarter. "Whatever that way is that we decide that week, we've got to play to it. That's what we're doing a good job of."

The Patriots were essentially flawless after disappearing into the locker room at halftime on uncertain terms. Coach Bill Belichick ordered a pair of kneel-downs to wipe out the final 51 seconds on the first half, despite being armed with three timeouts, after Brady's uncharacteristic pair of sloppy interceptions.

But the Pats scored touchdowns on their first four possessions after the break, all methodical drives that forced the Colts to press. Brady made amends for his first-half misfires by finding tight end Tim Wright in a tight window for a 2-yard

Patriots defensive end Dominique Easley gets to Indianapolis Colts quarterback Andrew Luck after he releases a second-quarter pass.

By Matt West / Boston Herald

Patriots quarterback Tom
Brady leaps onto tight end
Rob Gronkowski after a
fourth-quarter touchdown.
By Matt West / Boston Herald

touchdown that pushed the lead to 21-10.

The Colts could only muster a 53-yard field goal from Adam Vinatieri, thanks to Revis' third-and-6 tackle on receiver Reggie Wayne 1 yard shy of the sticks. Brady responded with two more third-down completions, hitting wideout Brandon LaFell for 26 yards and tight end Rob Gronkowski for 16, and Gray's 2-yard plunge made it 28-13 after three.

Luck hit offensive tackle Anthony Castonzo for a 1-yard touchdown to make it 28-20 early in the fourth, but the Patriots wouldn't let up, and Gray's 1-yard touchdown rebuilt the two-score lead with 8:43 remaining.

Completely unable to stop Brady and Gray, the Colts went for it on fourth-and-10 from their own 32, and Revis broke up Luck's bid for Wayne on the left sideline.

Gronkowski didn't have a gaudy statistical effort — four receptions, 71 yards, touchdown — but did bully his way for the exclamation point, breaking tackles and shoving aside defenders on a wild 26-yard score that capped the scoring and allowed Brady to spend the rest of the night resting on the sideline.

Brady's pair of first-half picks kept the Colts in the game. The second, 1:25 before the half,

Patriots running back Jonas Gray stiff-arms Indianapolis Colts strong safety Mike Adams in the first quarter.

By Matt West / Boston Herald

was an ill-fated, third-and-1 loft for Gronkowski. Safety Mike Adams' fair catch got the Colts in business at the Pats' 23, and three plays later, Luck cut the lead to 14-10 with a TD to receiver Hakeem Nicks.

"We let them back in there with kind of a dumb interception in the first half, but we came out and played a lot better in the second half," Brady said.

Gray wasted no time, rushing for 34 yards of the 77 the Pats piled up on their opening drive, capped with his 4-yard plunge through the junk for a 7-0 lead.

"It was definitely a tone-setter," Gray said of the opening drive.

After the Colts trimmed it to 7-3 with Vinatieri's 31-yard field goal, Brady completed a pair of third-down attempts on the ensuing drive, and Gray made it 14-3 with a 2-yard touchdown.

Aside from the two miscues from Brady, the Colts hardly got close enough again to make the Pats sweat.

"Bill asked for big plays to be made and for us to show up, and we did," defensive tackle Vince Wilfork said. "My hat goes off to everybody, the whole team. We played well." ▪

GAME STATISTICS

	New England	7	7	14	14	—	42
	Indianapolis	3	7	3	7	—	20

FIRST QUARTER

NE TD 8:37 Jonas Gray 4 Yd Run (Stephen Gostkowski Kick)
Drive: 11 plays, 89 yds, 4:14

IND FG 4:19 Adam Vinatieri 31 Yd Field Goal
Drive: 8 plays, 67 yds, 4:18

SECOND QUARTER

NE TD 3:50 Jonas Gray 2 Yd Run (Stephen Gostkowski Kick)
Drive: 11 plays, 68 yds, 4:36

IND TD 0:55 Hakeem Nicks 10 Yd pass from Andrew Luck (Adam Vinatieri Kick)
Drive: 3 plays, 23 yds, 0:21

THIRD QUARTER

NE TD 11:10 Tim Wright 2 Yd pass from Tom Brady (Stephen Gostkowski Kick)
Drive: 8 plays, 80 yds, 3:50

IND FG 8:31 Adam Vinatieri 53 Yd Field Goal
Drive: 6 plays, 40 yds, 2:39

NE TD 3:30 Jonas Gray 2 Yd Run (Stephen Gostkowski Kick)
Drive: 10 plays, 80 yds, 5:01

FOURTH QUARTER

IND TD 13:32 Anthony Castonzo 1 Yd pass from Andrew Luck (Adam Vinatieri Kick)
Drive: 11 plays, 80 yds, 4:58

NE TD 8:43 Jonas Gray 1 Yd Run (Stephen Gostkowski Kick)
Drive: 10 plays, 80 yds, 4:49

NE TD 6:46 Rob Gronkowski 26 Yd pass from Tom Brady (Stephen Gostkowski Kick)
Drive: 3 plays, 32 yds, 1:28

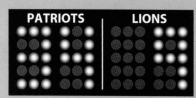
TEAM EFFORT

Pats show versatility in blowout

By JEFF HOWE | *Boston Herald*

The Patriots have been presented with all types of challenges during their seven-game winning streak.

Yesterday was the latest example of how they've conquered them all, as the Pats toppled the Lions, 34-9, at Gillette Stadium. The Patriots (9-2) posted the most points against the Lions' top-ranked defense this season, just one week after holding the Colts' No. 1 offense to a league low 20 points. And right before that, the Patriots dismantled the reigning AFC champion Broncos, who were viewed as the best team in the NFL.

The Patriots' chameleonic efforts have carried them to the conference's best record, as they passed on 53 of 73 plays yesterday. The week before, they compiled 250 rushing yards.

"No matter what situation we're going to be in, we're going to find a way to pull it out," Brandon LaFell said. "If we're going to run the ball or we're going to throw the ball, we're going to find a way to win. That's what good teams do."

Tom Brady completed 38-of-53 passes for 349 yards, two touchdowns and one interception, and he spread it to Julian Edelman (11 receptions, 89 yards), LaFell (nine receptions, 98 yards), Shane Vereen (eight receptions, 48 yards), Rob Gronkowski (five receptions, 78 yards) and Tim Wright (five receptions, 36 yards, two TDs).

LeGarrette Blount compiled 78 yards on 12 carries. Blount scored twice and had the bulk of the workload as Jonas Gray was evidently benched for being late Friday.

"(The Lions) played well," Blount said. "We just played better."

Surely, the Patriots took pride in their offensive distribution, but their most impressive performances might have come on the other side of the ball, as cornerbacks Darrelle Revis and Brandon Browner erased receivers Calvin Johnson and Golden Tate.

Quarterback Matthew Stafford (18-of-46, 264 yards, one interception) was 1-of-10 for 17 yards when

Detroit Lions running back Joique Bell is tackled
by a pack of Patriots in the third quarter.
By Nancy Lane / Boston Herald

targeting Revis, who forced nine consecutive incompletions to close the game.

The Pats defense, which also amassed two sacks, drew motivation by posting the Lions' rankings and some of their trash talk on a board in the meeting room throughout the week.

"We're always up for the challenge," Browner said. "All throughout the week, they had some of the comments that their defense said. Personally, we don't line up with their defense, but we took that as a challenge. You guys think you're the best, but we're confident that we can compete with the top defenses across the league."

Revis believed they were slighted by the Lions.

"I think a lot of us kind of viewed it as trash talk, too, of how they were just coming out of nowhere," Revis said. "I mean, they're the No. 1 defense. You've got to give them credit, too.

"At the same time, we know we've got a great defense, and we've got to continue to keep on pushing and working. We feel like we can match up with anybody across the board, and we feel like we can out-execute them."

Brady and the offense recovered from a 3-0 deficit and two three-and-outs by converting a pair of third

Patriots running back LeGarrette Blount is tackled by a pack of Lions in the third quarter.
By Nancy Lane / Boston Herald

downs on their third series. Brady hit Edelman for 10 yards on third-and-5 and hooked up with Wright for a 4-yard score that made it 7-3.

Revis defended an incompletion to Johnson in the end zone on the ensuing drive, which was capped by Matt Prater's 20-yard field goal, and Danny Amendola returned the following kickoff 81 yards to set up Blount's 3-yard score on his first carry of his second tour with the Patriots, which extended the lead to 14-6 in the second quarter.

Brady and Wright connected on third-and-goal for the second time on their next drive, as the 8-yarder was made possible by a Lions defense that swarmed Gronkowski. The Pats pushed the advantage to 24-6 at halftime after Gronk caught a pair of passes for 47 yards to set up Stephen Gostkowski's 35-yard field goal.

The Lions only mustered nine first downs in the second half and never forced the Pats to sweat. The Patriots closed the scoring with Blount's 1-yard plunge as the exclamation point of a third consecutive three-touchdown victory against a division leader. All required a different recipe. "It tells you that we go into the week ready to prepare and ready to work in practice. We have to continue to do that because every defense is a little different," Edelman said. "As long as we try to go out there each and every week and take in this preparation, what the coaches are harping on us for, we'll be all right." ▪

GAME STATISTICS

		Q1	Q2	Q3	Q4	Final
Detroit		3	3	0	3	— 9
New England		7	17	3	7	— 34

FIRST QUARTER

DET FG 11:44 Matt Prater 48 Yd Field Goal
Drive: 8 plays, 50 yds, 3:16

NE TD 3:10 Tim Wright 4 Yd pass from Tom Brady (Stephen Gostkowski Kick)
Drive: 9 plays, 64 yds, 2:37

SECOND QUARTER

DET FG 13:37 Matt Prater 20 Yd Field Goal
Drive: 10 plays, 78 yds, 4:33

NE TD 12:43 LeGarrette Blount 3 Yd Run (Stephen Gostkowski Kick)
Drive: 2 plays, 22 yds, 0:54

NE TD 2:42 Tim Wright 8 Yd pass from Tom Brady (Stephen Gostkowski Kick)
Drive: 13 plays, 93 yds, 5:03

NE FG 0:00 Stephen Gostkowski 35 Yd Field Goal
Drive: 4 plays, 40 yds, 0:35

THIRD QUARTER

NE FG 5:05 Stephen Gostkowski 43 Yd Field Goal
Drive: 9 plays, 50 yds, 3:27

FOURTH QUARTER

DET FG 14:48 Matt Prater 49 Yd Field Goal
Drive: 10 plays, 34 yds, 3:06

NE TD 1:53 LeGarrette Blount 1 Yd Run (Stephen Gostkowski Kick)
Drive: 9 plays, 66 yds, 4:30

Patriots defensive end Rob Ninkovich sacks Detroit Lions quarterback Matthew Stafford in the second quarter.
By Matt Stone / Boston Herald

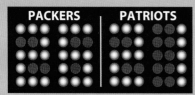

SHOUT IN THE COLD

Pats, Brady frustrated by missed opportunity

By JEFF HOWE | *Boston Herald*

Tom Brady's fervent outburst captured the Patriots' sentiment as he realized their fate in a 26-21 loss to the Packers yesterday at Lambeau Field.

Aaron Rodgers zipped one final throw through the narrowest of windows, finding Randall Cobb for 7 yards to convert on third-and-4 to eviscerate the remaining 2:28 and halt the Pats' impressive seven-game winning streak that victimized five teams that were at least division co-leaders. But Brady and company found no comfort in what had been done before their voyage to Lambeau. They only harped on what they allowed to slip away, and Brady's vibrant, profane tirade on the sideline epitomized their emotion in a difficult defeat.

"We really need to turn it up and just realize that every possession and every play is an opportunity," Brady said. "If you don't take advantage of it, you never know which play it's going to be in close games like this that leads to losses. We have to win tough games and find ways to make the important plays when we have them."

The Patriots (9-3) were a play away from stealing the potential Super Bowl preview and maintained their grasp of the AFC's top seed, but that offered little in an agitated locker room atmosphere.

"No such thing as a consolation," Brandon Browner said. "When you lose, you lose."

Rodgers completed 24-of-38 passes for 368 yards and two touchdowns, but he did the vast majority of his work by ignoring Darrelle Revis and Browner. Rodgers was 1-of-2 for 5 yards when targeting Browner and 2-of-6 for 53 yards and a touchdown when throwing at Revis, who surrendered a scoring grab for the first time since Week 1. Jordy Nelson caught a quick slant then blazed past Revis

Green Bay Packers wide receiver Jordy Nelson can't make a catch in the end zone defended by New England Patriots cornerback Darrelle Revis in the second quarter.
By Nancy Lane / Boston Herald

Patriots wide receiver Julian Edelman is taken down by Green Bay Packers inside linebacker Sam Barrington and free safety Micah Hyde in the second quarter.

By Nancy Lane / Boston Herald

and through Devin McCourty's angle for a pivotal 45-yard touchdown that made it 23-14 before halftime. Rodgers never looked Revis' way again.

"A loss is a bad taste in your mouth, especially if you're a competitor," Revis said. "I think I can speak for everybody in this locker room. We're all competitors.

"We want to win every game. That's damn right. I think that's why guys compete and why guys are in this business. You want to win. But at the same time, we played a great team today. We feel that we're a great team as well."

The Packers also set the pace from start to finish, scoring on their first five possessions and controlling the ball for 36:35 as they converted 10-of-17 third downs. The Patriots' red-zone defense, which yielded four field goals in four trips, kept them within striking distance after

quickly falling behind.

But Brady (22-of-35, 245 yards, two touchdowns) couldn't complete a challenging comeback. The Pats took over with 8:35 remaining, and Brady hooked up with Julian Edelman for 5 yards on fourth-and-3 near midfield and then found Rob Gronkowski for 10 yards on third-and-7 from the Packers' 43. Yet, Brady and Gronkowski couldn't complete a spectacular 20-yard connection in the end zone, as Ha Ha Clinton-Dix knocked the ball free from a diving Gronkowski on second-and-9.

"Pretty sure I caught it, and then at the last second, (Clinton-Dix) made a nice play," said Gronkowski, who led the Pats with seven catches for 98 yards. "He hit it out of my hand, so it was a good play by him. When my number is called, I've got to come down with those plays right there."

Then, the drive stalled when Nate Solder was

beaten for his first sack since Week 6, as Mike Daniels and Mike Neal closed in for a third-down Brady takedown. Stephen Gostkowski pushed a 47-yard field goal attempt with 2:40 to play, and Eddie Lacy (21 carries, 98 yards) and Rodgers finished the job.

While the Patriots took the loss hard, they certainly weren't letting it derail their focus with four regular-season games left.

"It's not always easy," Vince Wilfork said. "Playing at home and blowing out teams, and all of a sudden you've got to face a good football team on the road, it shows you what type of football team you really have. I think we have a damn good one."

The Pats opened conservatively after holding Mason Crosby to two field goals to open the game, as they punted on their first two series when faced with fourth-and-2 from their own 46-yard line and fourth-and-1 from their 49. Rodgers made them pay by dropping a dime to Richard Rodgers for a 32-yard touchdown over Patrick Chung to extend the lead to 13-0.

The Patriots finally fired back, as Brady connected with Gronkowski for 29 yards to kick-start an ensuing drive that culminated with Brandon Bolden's zigzagging 6-yard TD run that cut the margin to 13-7 with 12:59 remaining in the second quarter.

Dont'a Hightower's third-down sack brought about Crosby's 33-yard field goal and 16-7 advantage.

Brady kept it in high gear again, finding LaFell (five receptions, 38 yards, two touchdowns) for a 2-yard score to cut the deficit to 16-14 with 1:09 remaining in the second quarter before Nelson delivered a crucial blow with 14 seconds to go in the half.

It was the first time Revis had been beaten for a touchdown in 61 targets, but it kept the Pats at bay the rest of the night.

"He got a little separation with a push-off, but that's the game within the game," Revis said. "We're going to take this loss on the chin and go back to the drawing board and correct what we need to correct."∎

GAME STATISTICS

		New England	0	14	0	7	—	21
		Green Bay	13	10	0	3	—	26

FIRST QUARTER

GB	FG 11:14	Mason Crosby 32 Yd Field Goal **Drive:** 9 plays, 58 yds, 3:46
GB	FG 3:27	Mason Crosby 35 Yd Field Goal **Drive:** 11 plays, 66 yds, 5:49
GB	TD 0:08	Richard Rodgers 32 Yd pass from Aaron Rodgers (Mason Crosby Kick) **Drive:** 4 plays, 85 yds, 1:45

SECOND QUARTER

NE	TD 12:59	Brandon Bolden 6 Yd Run (Stephen Gostkowski Kick) **Drive:** 5 plays, 73 yds, 2:09
GB	FG 5:54	Mason Crosby 33 Yd Field Goal **Drive:** 13 plays, 57 yds, 7:05
NE	TD 1:09	Brandon LaFell 2 Yd pass from Tom Brady (Stephen Gostkowski Kick) **Drive:** 12 plays, 80 yds, 4:45
GB	TD 0:14	Jordy Nelson 45 Yd pass from Aaron Rodgers (Mason Crosby Kick) **Drive:** 5 plays, 81 yds, 0:55

FOURTH QUARTER

NE	TD 13:51	Brandon LaFell 15 Yd pass from Tom Brady (Stephen Gostkowski Kick) **Drive:** 9 plays, 78 yds, 3:30
GB	FG 8:41	Mason Crosby 28 Yd Field Goal **Drive:** 11 plays, 65 yds, 5:10

Patriots head coach Bill Belichick on the sidelines with quarterback Tom Brady in the third quarter.
By Nancy Lane / Boston Herald

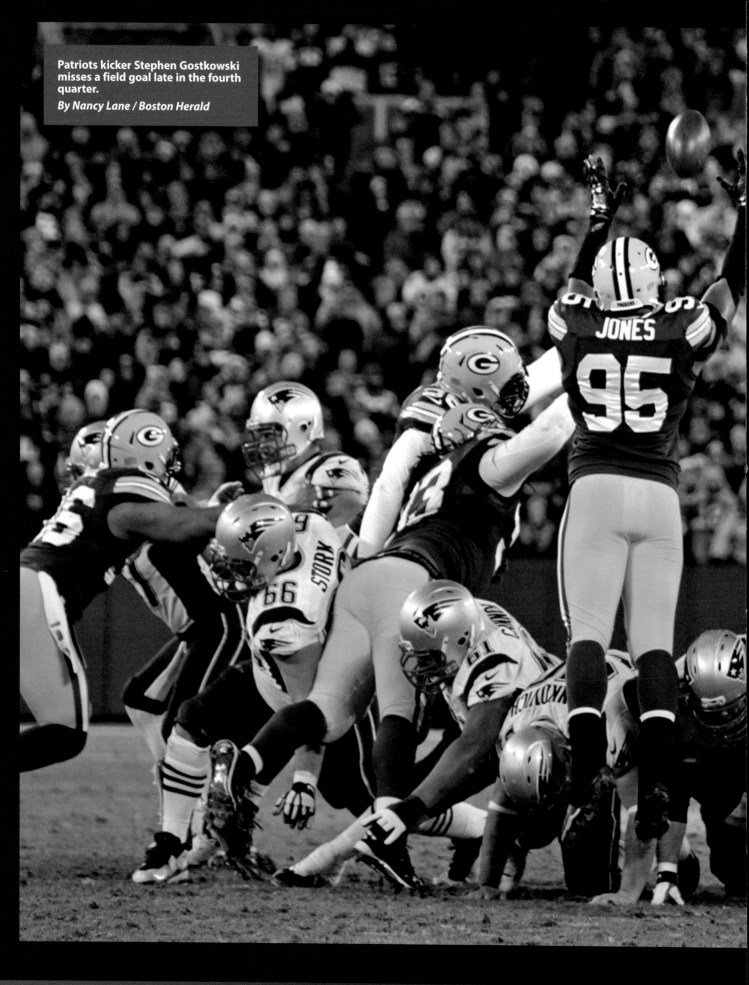

Patriots kicker Stephen Gostkowski misses a field goal late in the fourth quarter.

By Nancy Lane / Boston Herald

BILL BELICHICK

The faces of New England Patriots defensive tackle Vince Wilfork, head coach Bill Belichick and defensive assistant Brendan Daly tell the story as the Miami Dolphins take a 33-20 lead in the fourth quarter of the 2014 season-opener.
By Matt West / Boston Herald

Left: Belichick reacts in anger after a bad second-quarter play against the Kansas City Chiefs.
By Matt West / Boston Herald

BELICHICK BELONGS AMONG NFL'S COACHING GREATS

By RON BORGES | *Boston Herald*

Pro football is a concussive game of chess. It is a game of parrying and countering, of change and adjustment. Because of that, comparing eras always is difficult.

One of the game's most interesting aspects is its constant state of flux, an ongoing struggle for dominance between offense and defense. Yet for coaches, pro football remains what it has always been: a battle as much of wits as wallops.

Of the 473 head coaches in NFL history, only 22 have been inducted into the Pro Football Hall of Fame. In the opinion of most, those 22 are the game's greatest minds, and at some point, it's logical to assume Bill Belichick will join them.

Belichick waves to the crowd after thumping the Chicago Bears for a 51-23 victory.
By Matt West / Boston Herald

Belichick reacts to a Baltimore Ravens timeout on third down late in the game.

By Matt West / Boston Herald

When he does, the debate will rage about whether he's the greatest of them all. It's a debate with no easy answer.

The problems Vince Lombardi faced were far different than those Belichick tackles. Same would be true of George Halas or Bill Walsh, Don Shula or Curly Lambeau. In their days, once you built a team, you could maintain it because free agency did not exist. Then again, the same was true of their opponents, so you could argue their rivals remained stronger longer than Belichick's.

Such differences are one reason Steve Sabol, long-time president of NFL Films and a recognized historian of the game, contended Belichick was the finest coach of his time but avoided all-time. When someone has been coaching as long as Belichick (this is his 40th year in the NFL and 20th as a head coach), you have spanned the time from Paul Brown to Jim Harbaugh, so placing him in historic context covers a wide swath of the NFL's 94-year existence.

"He is to this century what Paul Brown was to the previous century," the late Sabol opined. "With the way he has built teams, his strategic

mind, the success he's had, he would be my easy choice (as coach of the decade)."

But what of all-time? One can argue all day about differences in eras, but at some point you have to go to the record because it is what it is. That's why it's impossible to beat Lombardi … because it was nearly impossible to beat Lombardi. In nine years with the Packers, Lombardi was 9-1 in the playoffs, winning five NFL titles (including the first two Super Bowls) in a seven-year stretch. Then he resurrected a long-dormant Redskins team in one year before dying of cancer. Hard to compete with that.

Belichick would be the first to tell you that in the innovation department, no coach rivaled Brown, who was 158-48-8 in his 17 years in Cleveland. At one point, he guided the Browns to 10 straight league championship games, winning six. Later, he left to create the Bengals, and in three years, they went from expansion team to playoff team. Add his inventions and innovations and it's difficult to dispute his prominent position among Hall of Fame coaches.

On the short list of other rivals, one comes to mind that might be overlooked. Washington's Joe

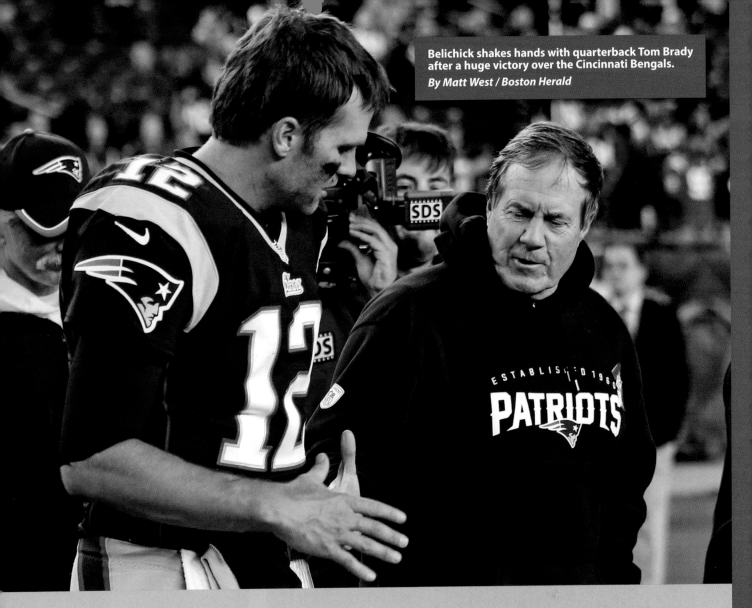

Belichick shakes hands with quarterback Tom Brady after a huge victory over the Cincinnati Bengals.
By Matt West / Boston Herald

Gibbs is the only coach to win three Super Bowls with three different quarterbacks. Had he not made an ill-advised comeback 12 years after retiring, his record would be 124-60. He did what the others could not. He won consistently without relying on a Hall of Famer running his offense.

Belichick has done his winning in the salary cap era, a restriction on team-building that requires an understanding of economics as well as football. Patriots owner Robert Kraft claims it was the former as much as the latter that attracted him to Belichick at a time when he was radioactive after his blustery failure in Cleveland. He now insists Belichick is the best of all-time.

So does one of Belichick's chief rivals. Speaking before last season's AFC title game, Peyton Manning called Belichick "the best coach I've ever competed against, and I think it's safe to say he'll go down as the greatest NFL coach of all time. (His) teams ... have always been well-coached, always been prepared, always played hard for 60 minutes. Those things jump out every single week, and to me that speaks to his coaching."

Belichick is a believer in situational football and opponent-specific game-planning well beyond the norm, and that has served him well as he enters this season ranked fifth all-time in victories (218) and third in winning percentage among coaches with at least 150 victories (.657), trailing only Halas and Shula. When it comes to the postseason, he has the seventh-best playoff record in history (19-9), trailing only Lombardi, Tom Flores, Walsh, Gibbs, John Harbaugh and Jimmy Johnson. How did this come about?

"I wouldn't say I was overly influenced by one person or another person," he once explained. "I was probably influenced a little bit by everybody. ... It's kind of a menagerie."

It's a menagerie that amalgamated into one of pro football's most successful coaching minds. ∎

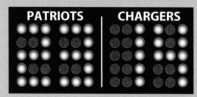

LATE CHARGE LOOMS LARGE

Brady's 'O' starts slow, finishes fast

By JEFF HOWE | *Boston Herald*

For a while last night, it appeared the Patriots weren't going to fondly remember their week at the beach.

But they turned on the jets in the fourth quarter to dispose of the San Diego Chargers, 23-14, at Qualcomm Stadium and maintain control of the AFC's No. 1 seed. The Pats (10-3) can win a sixth consecutive AFC East title next Sunday with a victory against the Miami Dolphins at Gillette Stadium.

The Pats were elated the week in San Diego paid off after a tense loss to the Packers.

"Everybody had their head down ready to work, and it showed tonight," defensive tackle Vince Wilfork said. "That's a big win for us as a team."

Linebacker Jamie Collins, cornerback Darrelle Revis and the defense carried the team for much of the night until Tom Brady's bunch finally seized control. Collins led the Pats with two sacks and nine tackles, and Revis held quarterback Philip Rivers to a 3-yard completion on his only target toward The Island in the game.

After allowing the Packers to race around the field on third down (10-of-17), the Patriots limited the Chargers to four conversions on 13 attempts. The Chargers only had 13 first downs and 216 offensive yards.

"I think (coach) Bill (Belichick) did a great job," Revis said. "I think this was key during our season this year to do something like this coming off a big game last week where we lost. It was devastating for us, but at the same time, I think we had a great time out here just team bonding and everybody sticking together coming off that loss."

With San Diego Chargers inside linebacker Donald Butler hot on his tail Patriots wide receiver Julian Edelman runs 69 yards for a touchdown during the fourth quarter.
By Matt Stone / Boston Herald

San Diego Chargers quarterback Philip Rivers chases down New England Patriots free safety Devin McCourty as he dives in for a touchdown that was called back for a penalty during the third quarter.
By Matt Stone / Boston Herald

Stephen Gostkowski's 38-yard field goal gave the Pats the lead at 16-14 with 10:34 remaining in the fourth quarter, and wide receiver Julian Edelman (eight catches, 141 yards) broke it open two minutes later.

After the Chargers' fourth three-and-out of the game, Brady connected with Edelman on a crossing pattern, and Edelman broke tackles by safety Marcus Gilchrist and cornerback Brandon Flowers to race away with a 69-yard touchdown that made it 23-14.

"That was awesome," said tight end Rob Gronkowski, who, with eight catches for 87 yards and a touchdown, became the first tight end in history with four 10-TD seasons. "You've got to give huge props to (Edelman) on that catch and run, unbelievable, and a good throw by Tom. He was due to break one out, and it was awesome to see it."

For much of the game, the Patriots were playing from behind.

San Diego's first score came early in the second quarter when wide receiver Malcom Floyd beat cornerback Brandon Browner on a double move on third-and-7 and hauled in a 15-yard TD pass.

Brady, who was 28-of-44 for 317 yards, two touchdowns and one interception, got the Patriots moving in the right direction on their ensuing

series and hit receiver Brandon LaFell for a potential third-down conversion, but Jahleel Addae stripped the ball and fellow safety Darrell Stuckey returned it 53 yards to the house for a 14-3 lead.

But the Chargers only scored once in 12 possessions, which essentially negated the early adversity.

"You've got to fight," Browner said. "You've got to fight for 60 minutes. We thought it shouldn't have even been that close, but that's a good football team we just beat. They were fighting until the end, and we fought until the end and we came out with the 'W.'"

The Pats' red-zone woes continued on their next possession, as Brady threw incompletions into tight coverage on second- and third-and-goal from the 4, which resulted in Gostkowski's second 22-yard field goal, which trimmed the deficit to 14-6.

After the defense held the Chargers to their first three-and-out, Brandon Bolden beat UConn product Donald Brown around the edge of the formation and blocked Mike Scifres' punt to set up the Patriots at the Chargers' 25-yard line.

Four plays later, Brady connected with Gronkowski for a 14-yard touchdown that cut the margin to 14-13 with 3:30 left in the half.

The Patriots had a chance to take the lead before the break, but another strange second-

Patriots guard Dan Connolly and wide receiver Julian Edelman celebrate tight end Rob Gronkowski's touchdown during the second quarter.

By Matt Stone / Boston Herald

quarter decision, Brady's second in the last four weeks, doomed that opportunity. The Patriots took over with 1:32 to play and moved 43 yards to the Chargers' 18 before Brady was pressured on second down. He lofted a bid for Gronkowski by the left sideline of the end zone, but linebacker Manti Te'o picked off the under-thrown ball at the 4-yard line.

The Pats appeared to take the lead midway through the third quarter when safety Devin McCourty returned an interception 56 yards for a touchdown after Browner's wicked shoulder-to-shoulder hit dislodged a bouncing ball from receiver Ladarius Green's grasp. However, Browner was flagged for unnecessary roughness to negate the score.

Though it was a questionable penalty, the Patriots universally said the big hit fired up the team.

"Leading with my shoulder, most definitely, targeting his numbers," Browner said. ∎

GAME STATISTICS

	1	2	3	4	—	Total
New England	3	10	0	10	—	23
San Diego	0	14	0	0	—	14

FIRST QUARTER
NE FG 3:15 — Stephen Gostkowski 22 Yd Field Goal
Drive: 17 plays, 89 yds, 7:56

SECOND QUARTER
SD TD 13:29 — Malcom Floyd 15 Yd pass from Philip Rivers (Nick Novak Kick)
Drive: 11 plays, 80 yds, 4:46

SD TD 11:06 — Darrell Stuckey 53 Yd Fumble Return (Nick Novak Kick)
Drive: 4 plays, 28 yds, 2:23

NE FG 7:38 — Stephen Gostkowski 22 Yd Field Goal
Drive: 12 plays, 70 yds, 3:28

NE TD 3:28 — Rob Gronkowski 14 Yd pass from Tom Brady (Stephen Gostkowski Kick)
Drive: 4 plays, 25 yds, 2:03

FOURTH QUARTER
NE FG 10:34 — Stephen Gostkowski 38 Yd Field Goal
Drive: 10 plays, 55 yds, 5:04

NE TD 8:41 — Julian Edelman 69 Yd pass from Tom Brady (Stephen Gostkowski Kick)
Drive: 1 plays, 69 yds, 0:12

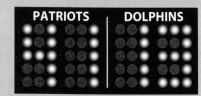
DIVISION OF COWER

Pats collect another title, silence Fish

By JEFF HOWE | *Boston Herald*

Quite often over the past decade and a half, the AFC East race essentially ended when Tom Brady put on his jersey and Bill Belichick pulled the hoodie over his head.

The Patriots, who claimed their 12th division crown in the last 14 years yesterday with a 41-13 victory against Miami at Gillette Stadium, took exception to some of the Dolphins' loud confidence this week, to the point where they discussed it every day at the facility. The Pats wanted the Dolphins to feel like Week 1 was such a distant memory that it could have been confused with 2008.

"It was a lot of talk," Darrelle Revis said. "Those guys were chirping. The Miami Dolphins were chirping this week about they should have beat us by 50 and all of those type of things in the first game. If that's what they want to do, that's what they want to do. The one thing you've got to understand is you get a second stab at it because we're in the same (division), so you might need to watch what you say."

The Pats (11-3) handed the Dolphins (7-7) their most lopsided loss since 2012 and strengthened their hold on the AFC's No. 1 seed. They've won 9 of 10 games since an embarrassing defeat to the Kansas City Chiefs and can secure a first-round bye next Sunday by beating the New York Jets.

"We've been in some tough situations, and we fought through them as a team should," Vince Wilfork said. "A good team should fight through some stuff, and we did."

Offensive coordinator Josh McDaniels uncorked a fiery halftime speech to get the Pats in order after a disappointing pair of quarters, and Brady took over from there.

Brady, who has won more division titles than any starting quarterback in history, completed 21-of-35 passes for 287 yards, two touchdowns and one interception, but he was 13-of-20 for 205 yards and both scores when the Pats dismantled the Dolphins in the second half. Julian Edelman led the way with seven catches for 88 yards and a score, and Rob Gronkowski added three catches for 96 yards and a touchdown, all of which occurred after the break.

Patriots strong safety Duron Harmon is cheered on by Pat the Patriot as he runs with a first-quarter interception.

By Matt West / Boston Herald

Patriots wide receiver Danny Amendola returns the opening kickoff in the third quarter.

By Matt West / Boston Herald

"I'm glad we started to earn our paycheck there in the second half," Brady said. "It was good to be able to do that. It was a good feeling."

Brady and Gronkowski opened the third quarter with a 34-yard connection, and Brady further sparked the Pats with a 17-yard scramble on third-and-11. He juked Philip Wheeler with a pump fake and lowered his shoulder into Walt Aikens on the sideline before hopping back to his feet to unleash a rebel yell.

"I was going to slide," Brady said, "but I was pretty pissed off."

LeGarrette Blount closed the drive with a 3-yard touchdown to make it 21-13. Stephen Gostkowski capped the ensuing possession with a 35-yard field goal that pushed the margin to 24-13 and made him the franchise's all-time leading scorer, as he passed Adam Vinatieri (1,158 points).

But the Patriots really began piling on from there, as Brandon Browner lit up Lamar Miller as the running back tried to corral a pass over the middle. Patrick Chung intercepted the deflected ball, and Brady hit Gronkowski for a 27-yard touchdown to extend the lead to 31-13 one play later.

After the Dolphins followed with a three-and-out, Brady and Gronkowski stepped on the pedal again with a 35-yard connection to set up Edelman's 6-yard scoring grab on the following play to make it 38-13 and put the finishing touches on a franchise-record 24-point third quarter.

Gostkowski added a 36-yard field goal in the fourth quarter to finish the scoring, as the Patriots capped their fourth straight game of not allowing a second-half touchdown and enjoyed silencing their noisy division rivals.

"We play on the field, not in the media," Wilfork said. "The game is always won between the lines."

The Patriots closed the first half with a three-phase meltdown to let the Dolphins back in the game. After taking over at their own 15-yard line with 40 seconds remaining in the second quarter, Shane Vereen ran three times for 2 yards to wipe out 15 seconds as the Dolphins used three timeouts.

Jarvis Landry then evaded a few tackles to return Ryan Allen's punt 32 yards to the Pats 32. With 11 seconds remaining, Ryan Tannehill (29-of-47, 346 yards, touchdown, two interceptions) immediately attacked Malcolm Butler in a one-on-

Patriots running back LeGarrette Blount celebrates his third quarter touchdown with the Minutemen.

By Matt West / Boston Herald

one matchup against Mike Wallace, who easily strode past his assignment down the left sideline for a 32-yard score to cut the deficit to 14-13.

"That's something we definitely don't want to do," Revis said of the late touchdown. "That's a headache for everybody on defense, including the coaches. That's not how we want to play."

In the second half, they showed the Dolphins how.∎

Patriots head coach Bill Belichick gets a hug from quarterback Tom Brady after clinching the AFC East title with a 41-13 victory over the Miami Dolphins.

By Matt West / Boston Herald

GAME STATISTICS

			Miami	3	10	0	0	—	13
			New England	7	7	24	3	—	41

FIRST QUARTER

NE — TD — 12:36 — Kyle Arrington 62 Yd Return of Blocked Field Goal (Stephen Gostkowski Kick)
Drive: 5 plays, 57 yds, 2:24

MIA — FG — 0:59 — Caleb Sturgis 24 Yd Field Goal
Drive: 9 plays, 60 yds, 4:47

SECOND QUARTER

NE — TD — 7:59 — Shane Vereen 3 Yd Run (Stephen Gostkowski Kick)
Drive: 3 plays, 8 yds, 0:42

MIA — FG — 4:26 — Caleb Sturgis 53 Yd Field Goal
Drive: 7 plays, 38 yds, 3:33

MIA — TD — 0:05 — Mike Wallace 32 Yd pass from Ryan Tannehill (Caleb Sturgis Kick)
Drive: 1 plays, 32 yds, 0:06

THIRD QUARTER

NE — TD — 11:04 — LeGarrette Blount 3 Yd Run (Stephen Gostkowski Kick)
Drive: 8 plays, 79 yds, 3:56

NE — FG — 4:43 — Stephen Gostkowski 35 Yd Field Goal
Drive: 10 plays, 47 yds, 4:03

NE — TD — 4:30 — Rob Gronkowski 27 Yd pass from Tom Brady (Stephen Gostkowski Kick)
Drive: 1 plays, 27 yds, 0:05

NE — TD — 1:29 — Julian Edelman 6 Yd pass from Tom Brady (Stephen Gostkowski Kick)
Drive: 3 plays, 47 yds, 1:19

FOURTH QUARTER

NE — FG — 6:20 — Stephen Gostkowski 36 Yd Field Goal
Drive: 11 plays, 67 yds, 4:26

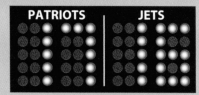

PATRIOTS   JETS

PATS JUST GET BYE

Next goal: home–field advantage

By JEFF HOWE | *Boston Herald*

The Patriots played like a team that could use a week off during yesterday's 17-16 squeaker over the New York Jets at MetLife Stadium.

And this season, they have also performed to the level of a team that deserved that break, as the Pats (12-3) secured a first-round bye for an NFL-record fifth consecutive year. The Patriots have won 10 of their last 11 games and will lock up the AFC's No. 1 seed as early as tonight if the Cincinnati Bengals beat the Denver Broncos. Otherwise, the Pats can lock up the top seed next Sunday by beating the Buffalo Bills or if the Broncos fall to the Oakland Raiders.

"Go Bengals," defensive end Rob Ninkovich said.

The Pats expected a hard-nosed battle with their division rivals in what figured to be the final home game of Rex Ryan's career as Jets coach, and that's what they got. Tom Brady was sacked four times in the first half as the Patriots suited up without left guard Dan Connolly (knee) or the always reliable receiver Julian Edelman (concussion), and the quarterback completed 23-of-35 passes for 182 yards, a touchdown and an interception while getting hit 11 times.

Brady nearly had a crucial mistake in the fourth quarter but was rescued by the defense and special teams. Clinging to a 17-16 lead, the 37-year-old was drilled by linebacker Jason Babin with 7:26 remaining, which yielded a wild throw behind receiver Brandon LaFell, who reached back for the ball but inadvertently deflected it to cornerback Marcus Williams for an interception at the 30-yard line.

Three plays later, Pats linebacker Dont'a Hightower converged on Jets quarterback Geno Smith for a third-down sack and 10-yard loss. Defensive tackle Vince Wilfork — or, "Air Wilfork," according to safety Devin

Patriots quarterback Tom Brady is sacked in the first quarter by New York Jets inside linebacker Demario Davis and defensive back Antonio Allen, left.

By Matt West / Boston Herald

Patriots running back Jonas Gray goes over New York Jets strong safety Dawan Landry for a fourth-quarter touchdown.
By Matt West / Boston Herald

McCourty — then pushed through the line to block Nick Folk's 52-yard field-goal attempt with 5:21 to play. It was the same pre-snap shift that the Patriots used when defensive lineman Chris Jones blocked Folk's 58-yarder to seal a Week 7 win.

"I felt that I had a good shot of getting some penetration, so it worked out well," Wilfork said of the franchise-record fourth blocked field-goal attempt this season. "I'm glad I helped my team win a ball game. That's what it's all about."

The Patriots then evaporated the final 5:16 of regulation, as Brady completed 3-of-4 passes for 26 yards and Brandon Bolden rushed four times for 29 yards.

"It's the Jets and the Patriots. That team right there, their record, if you're outside looking in, we should have rolled those guys," cornerback Brandon Browner said. "But we knew going in this was going to be a tough battle regardless, and it came down to exactly what we thought it would be — a tight football game, and the last drive of the game, we ran the clock out to win the game."

The Patriots have outscored their last six opponents, 92-22, in the second half, and they haven't allowed a touchdown after the break since Week 11. The strong finish helped them survive an ugly first half in which they only converted 1-of-5 third downs and amassed 9 rushing yards on six carries. The Pats didn't crack midfield in a scoreless first quarter and went three-and-out three times in the opening half.

Defensively, the Patriots allowed four scoring drives of at least 10 plays, so the Jets won the time-of-possession battle (32:21-27:39) for the second time this season.

"We're playing good football right now, but we've got one more week to get where we want to go to, get this bye and clinch homefield advantage," Browner said.

Receiver Danny Amendola, who had season highs with eight catches for 63 yards, set up the Pats' first score with a 39-yard punt return, and Brady found tight end Rob Gronkowski (six catches, 31 yards) in the left corner of the end zone for a 3-yard touchdown and 7-0 lead early in the second.

Smith answered the Gronkowski score when he hit tight end Jeff Cumberland for a 20-yard touchdown. Folk's 26-yard field goal gave the Jets a 10-7 advantage with 52 seconds remaining in the half, then another gave them a 13-7 lead in the third.

The Pats revived their running game on the next series. Shane Vereen ran six times for 38 yards, but the Pats stalled at the 6-yard line and settled for Stephen Gostkowski's 24-yard field goal to trim the deficit to 13-10.

Smith's next offering was sabotaged by defensive end Chandler Jones' crunching hit, and linebacker Jamie Collins intercepted the underthrow to set up the offense at the 38-yard line. Jonas Gray's 1-yard plunge gave the Patriots a 17-13 lead with 13:51 left.

A Folk 37-yard field goal on the next drive made it a 17-16 game.

"It's great," cornerback Darrelle Revis said. "It was tough today. These games come down to this, especially with this rivalry with the Pats and Jets, and we fought hard."∎

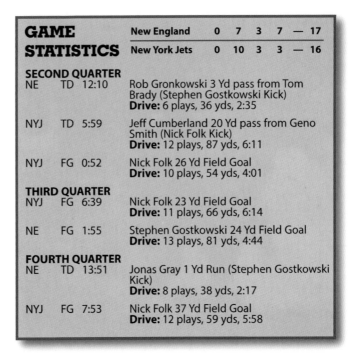

GAME STATISTICS		New England	0	7	3	7	—	17
		New York Jets	0	10	3	3	—	16

SECOND QUARTER

NE	TD	12:10	Rob Gronkowski 3 Yd pass from Tom Brady (Stephen Gostkowski Kick) **Drive:** 6 plays, 36 yds, 2:35
NYJ	TD	5:59	Jeff Cumberland 20 Yd pass from Geno Smith (Nick Folk Kick) **Drive:** 12 plays, 87 yds, 6:11
NYJ	FG	0:52	Nick Folk 26 Yd Field Goal **Drive:** 10 plays, 54 yds, 4:01

THIRD QUARTER

NYJ	FG	6:39	Nick Folk 23 Yd Field Goal **Drive:** 11 plays, 66 yds, 6:14
NE	FG	1:55	Stephen Gostkowski 24 Yd Field Goal **Drive:** 13 plays, 81 yds, 4:44

FOURTH QUARTER

NE	TD	13:51	Jonas Gray 1 Yd Run (Stephen Gostkowski Kick) **Drive:** 8 plays, 38 yds, 2:17
NYJ	FG	7:53	Nick Folk 37 Yd Field Goal **Drive:** 12 plays, 59 yds, 5:58

Left: Patriots cornerback Brandon Browner celebrates a 17-16 victory over the New York Jets.
By Matt West / Boston Herald

Below: Patriots outside linebacker Dont'a Hightower sacks New York Jets quarterback Geno Smith in the fourth quarter, taking the Jets further away from an easy field goal.
By Matt West / Boston Herald

Patriots defensive tackle Vince Wilfork gets a hand on New York Jets kicker Nick Folk's field goal attempt for a block in the fourth quarter.

By Matt West / Boston Herald

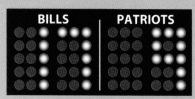

BILLS   PATRIOTS

REGULAR SEASON
> GAME 16
Dec. 28, 2014
BILLS @ PATRIOTS

HALF-HEARTED EFFORT

Stars play limited role in Pats loss

By JEFF HOWE | *Boston Herald*

And on the seventh day of the 17th week, Tom Brady remained healthy, so the Patriots rejoiced.

Aside from that, the Pats had an uneventful regular-season finale yesterday at Gillette Stadium, where the Buffalo Bills departed with a 17-9 victory. The Patriots (12-4), as the AFC's No. 1 seed who had little to play for beyond pride, now turn their full attention toward the playoffs.

The Pats will conduct a series of practices during the bye week before opening the postseason on Saturday, Jan. 10, at 4:30 p.m.

"Some of the goals are accomplished, but we're nowhere near the ultimate goal," wide receiver Brandon LaFell said. "We're just getting started."

Quarterback Tom Brady completed 8-of-16 passes for 80 yards in the first half and left the game trailing 17-6. Defensive backs Darrelle Revis and Devin McCourty and linebacker Jamie Collins also got the quick hook with Brady, while tight end Rob Gronkowski (healthy scratch), receiver Julian Edelman (concussion), tackle Sebastian Vollmer (back), guard Dan Connolly (knee), linebacker Dont'a Hightower (shoulder) and cornerback Brandon Browner (groin) were inactive for maintenance purposes. Cornerback Kyle Arrington (hamstring) was also given the day off despite being in uniform.

As a result, it was a lackadaisical type of day at Gillette, resembling a preseason affair. Still, the Pats' latest slow start continued a troubling trend, as they've been outscored, 77-54, in the first half of the last five games. The defense hasn't allowed a second-half touchdown since Week 11 to mask those early deficiencies.

"We have a lot of confidence as an offense," Brady said. "We've been able to score points against a lot of good teams, a lot of good defenses. Nothing that we've done

Buffalo Bills cornerback Ron Brooks tackles New England Patriots wide receiver Brandon LaFell in the third quarter.
By Matt Stone / Boston Herald

Patriots quarterback Jimmy
Garoppolo dives in for some
extra yards in the third quarter.
By Matt Stone / Boston Herald

this past season is going to help in two weeks
from now."

The Patriots did suffer one concerning injury,
as tackle Nate Solder tweaked his right knee on
the third-to-last snap of the first half and did not
return. LaFell returned after briefly leaving with a
left leg injury in the fourth quarter, and defensive
lineman Sealver Siliga said he was fine after
departing late in the fourth with an unknown
ailment.

"When there are games like this and we've
already got our playoffs situated, already got the
seed situated, for us to not get anybody injured,
that's a plus," LaFell said.

Backup quarterback Jimmy Garoppolo, who
took over in the third quarter, made some nice
plays while scrambling for his life behind a
patchwork offensive line, but he couldn't spark a
comeback. Garoppolo completed 10-of-17 passes
for 90 yards, rushed four times for 16 yards and
led a five-play, 27-yard drive that yielded Stephen
Gostkowski's 35-yard field goal for the 17-9 final.

Garoppolo and the Pats had one more

opportunity after taking over at their own 25-yard
line with 1:50 remaining in the fourth quarter, but
they couldn't gain a first down.

"It was a good experience, getting out there and
actually getting in (instead of) a preseason game,"
Garoppolo said. "Getting some live reps will only
help going forward."

Bills quarterback Kyle Orton drove the Bills
down the field for an easy touchdown on the
game's opening series. Revis barely missed a
diving pass breakup against receiver Sammy
Watkins, who gained 43 yards to set up the score.
Two plays later, Orton hit Robert Woods for a 6-
yard touchdown and 7-0 lead after a breakdown in
defensive communication left the receiver wide
open in the end zone.

"We didn't play to our standards," said Revis,
who only allowed the one catch on two targets.

The Pats trimmed the deficit to 7-3 with
Gostkowski's 24-yard field goal after the goal-to-go
opportunity stalled at the 6-yard line.

But the Bills kept charging with a 13-play, 80-
yard touchdown march that was capped by

Patriots wide receiver Danny Amendola dives over Buffalo Bills linebacker Ty Powell during a kick return in the third quarter.

By Matt Stone / Boston Herald

running back Boobie Dixon's 1-yard touchdown plunge on third-and-goal, making it 14-3.

Collins helped set up the Pats' second score by beating running back C.J. Spiller twice to strip-sack Orton and then diving through the pile to recover the fumble at the Bills 44-yard line. Gostkowski later trimmed the margin to 14-6 with a 44-yard field goal.

Dan Carpenter's 48-yard field goal extended the Bills' lead to 17-6 with 2:14 remaining in the half, and the starters' final bid on a two-minute drill yielded a single first down.

"We'll have a bad taste in our mouth until we get a chance to play again," guard Ryan Wendell said. ∎

GAME STATISTICS

			Buffalo	7	10	0	0	—	17
			New England	3	3	3	0	—	9

FIRST QUARTER

BUF   TD   11:59   Robert Woods 6 Yd pass from Kyle Orton (Dan Carpenter Kick)
Drive: 6 plays, 80 yds, 3:01

NE   FG   3:02   Stephen Gostkowski 24 Yd Field Goal
Drive: 13 plays, 80 yds, 5:33

SECOND QUARTER

BUF   TD   10:38   Boobie Dixon 1 Yd Run (Dan Carpenter Kick)
Drive: 13 plays, 80 yds, 7:24

NE   FG   5:07   Stephen Gostkowski 44 Yd Field Goal
Drive: 8 plays, 18 yds, 3:24

BUF   FG   2:14   Dan Carpenter 48 Yd Field Goal
Drive: 7 plays, 17 yds, 2:53

THIRD QUARTER

NE   FG   0:37   Stephen Gostkowski 35 Yd Field Goal
Drive: 5 plays, 27 yds, 2:18

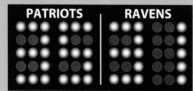

OLD FAMILIAR PLACE

Brady leads Pats into 4th straight AFC title game

By JEFF HOWE | *Boston Herald*

This season has been a throwback to the glory years for Tom Brady and the Patriots, and they mimicked some of their all-time great postseason performances at Gillette Stadium.

The Patriots became the first team to overcome two 14-point deficits in knocking off the Baltimore Ravens, 35-31, to advance to their fourth consecutive AFC Championship game. The winner of today's Denver Broncos vs. Indianapolis Colts matchup will visit Gillette Stadium next Sunday.

The Pats leaned on Brady once again, as he led the 46th game-winning drive of his career, including his eighth in the playoffs. The 37-year-old completed 8-of-9 passes for 71 yards on the game-winning drive, and he hit Brandon LaFell for a 23-yard touchdown in the left corner of the end zone with 5:13 to play.

"You don't want to say you expect that, but it's Tom Brady," said Julian Edelman, who had eight catches for 74 yards. "It's always nice to have that guy."

Duron Harmon essentially sealed it with a pick in the end zone with 1:39 to play, but the Ravens had one more prayer. However, Joe Flacco's 52-yard Hail Mary was knocked down by Devin McCourty in the end zone.

"The best thing is just give everybody credit on this team, coaching staff-wise, player-wise, of not going in the tank," Darrelle Revis said. "A lot of teams probably would go in the tank being down by two touchdowns. During the season, we've been through some ups and downs as well. We just persevered through them."

Brady started slow but finished 33-of-50 for 367 yards, three TDs and one interception to outduel Flacco, who was 28-of-45 for 292 yards, four scores and two picks.

A Patriots fan screams before the AFC Divisional playoff game against the Baltimore Ravens.
By Matt Stone / Boston Herald

Patriots strong safety Duron Harmon intercepts a late fourth-quarter pass intended for Baltimore Ravens wide receiver Torrey Smith which would have been a go-ahead touchdown.
By Matt West / Boston Herald

The Patriots clawed their way back from a 14-0 deficit but gave it right back with some crucial errors. Brady forced an underthrown ball to Rob Gronkowski (seven catches, 108 yards, TD) up the middle, and Daryl Smith intercepted it to set up the Ravens at their 43 with 1:03 remaining in the first half.

Four plays later, Revis was hit for a pass interference flag after exchanging hand checks with Steve Smith up the right sideline, and the 20-yard penalty put the Ravens at the Pats' 24. Flacco then gave the Ravens a 21-14 lead with 10 seconds to play in the half when he delivered an 11-yard strike to Owen Daniels.

The Pats opened the third quarter with a three-and-out, and the Ravens went on attack mode. Torrey Smith beat Brandon Browner for 35 yards on fourth-and-6, and Flacco hit Justin Forsett on a swing pass for an untouched 16-yard score that extended the lead to 28-14.

The Patriots fought back yet again with a nine-play, 80-yard drive that didn't require a third down but utilized three trick plays with just four offensive linemen. Brady and Gronkowski connected for a 5-yard touchdown to trim the lead in half, 28-21, with 6:48 to go in the third.

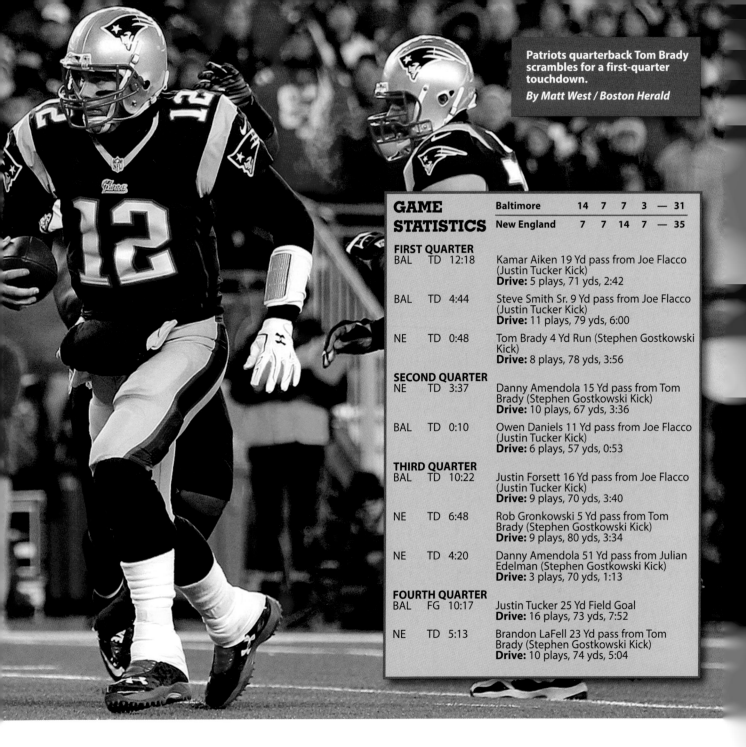

Patriots quarterback Tom Brady scrambles for a first-quarter touchdown.

By Matt West / Boston Herald

GAME STATISTICS

	1	2	3	4		T
Baltimore	14	7	7	3	—	31
New England	7	7	14	7	—	35

FIRST QUARTER
BAL TD 12:18 Kamar Aiken 19 Yd pass from Joe Flacco (Justin Tucker Kick)
Drive: 5 plays, 71 yds, 2:42

BAL TD 4:44 Steve Smith Sr. 9 Yd pass from Joe Flacco (Justin Tucker Kick)
Drive: 11 plays, 79 yds, 6:00

NE TD 0:48 Tom Brady 4 Yd Run (Stephen Gostkowski Kick)
Drive: 8 plays, 78 yds, 3:56

SECOND QUARTER
NE TD 3:37 Danny Amendola 15 Yd pass from Tom Brady (Stephen Gostkowski Kick)
Drive: 10 plays, 67 yds, 3:36

BAL TD 0:10 Owen Daniels 11 Yd pass from Joe Flacco (Justin Tucker Kick)
Drive: 6 plays, 57 yds, 0:53

THIRD QUARTER
BAL TD 10:22 Justin Forsett 16 Yd pass from Joe Flacco (Justin Tucker Kick)
Drive: 9 plays, 70 yds, 3:40

NE TD 6:48 Rob Gronkowski 5 Yd pass from Tom Brady (Stephen Gostkowski Kick)
Drive: 9 plays, 80 yds, 3:34

NE TD 4:20 Danny Amendola 51 Yd pass from Julian Edelman (Stephen Gostkowski Kick)
Drive: 3 plays, 70 yds, 1:13

FOURTH QUARTER
BAL FG 10:17 Justin Tucker 25 Yd Field Goal
Drive: 16 plays, 73 yds, 7:52

NE TD 5:13 Brandon LaFell 23 Yd pass from Tom Brady (Stephen Gostkowski Kick)
Drive: 10 plays, 74 yds, 5:04

After forcing a quick three-and-out, the Patriots knotted the score when offensive coordinator Josh McDaniels reached deeper into his bag of tricks. Brady threw laterally to Julian Edelman, who then unleashed the first pass of his Patriots career and hit a streaking Danny Amendola in stride for a 51-yard touchdown with 4:20 remaining in the third.

"I'm happy it got executed because that means I've got a life to maybe throw again," Edelman cracked.

The Pats then missed chances to really take over. McCourty's interception on the ensuing drive put Brady on the Ravens 37, but the QB threw three consecutive incompletions.

Three plays later, Jamie Collins strip-sacked Flacco and recovered the fumble at the Ravens 4, but Revis was flagged for defensive holding. The Ravens turned that into a 16-play, 73-yard march that erased 7:52 and resulted in Justin Tucker's 25-yard field goal that made it 31-28 with 10:17 to play.

That's when Brady took over.

"He's a great quarterback," Revis said. "He makes plays. I don't know what to tell you. He is clutch. He is very clutch."∎

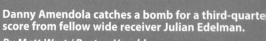

Danny Amendola catches a bomb for a third-quarter score from fellow wide receiver Julian Edelman.

By Matt West / Boston Herald

Wide receiver Julian Edelman rears back to throw after catching a lateral pass from Tom Brady.

By Matt West / Boston Herald, above
By Matt Stone / Boston Herald, right

Danny Amendola hugs Julian Edelman after the two connected on a touchdown pass from Edelman.

By Matt West / Boston Herald

Patriots nose tackle Alan Branch and defensive end Chandler Jones can't knock down Baltimore Ravens kicker Justin Tucker's field goal during the fourth quarter.

By Matt Stone / Boston Herald

A slew of Patriots defenders fights to prevent a Hail Mary attempt in the end zone by the Baltimore Ravens.

By Matt West / Boston Herald

Patriots legends Troy Brown,
Tedy Bruschi and Ty Law have
a great time with team owner
Robert Kraft before the game.
By Nancy Lane / Boston Herald

Fans show their support of Gronk at the AFC Championship game.
By Matt Stone / Boston Herald

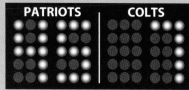

MORE HORSEPOWER

Pats flatten Colts, off to Super Bowl

By JEFF HOWE | *Boston Herald*

The Patriots will head to the desert in search of their first Super Bowl victory in a decade.

The Pats drubbed the Indianapolis Colts, 45-7, last night at Gillette Stadium to win their sixth AFC Championship game of the Bill Belichick era. They'll meet the Seattle Seahawks in Super Bowl XLIX in Glendale, Ariz., on Feb. 1.

"I only have one thing to say: We're on to Seattle," said Belichick, who set an NFL record with his 21st playoff victory.

Quarterback Tom Brady will set his own mark with his sixth Super Bowl start after schooling young buck Andrew Luck and the Colts for the fourth time in four meetings. Once again, it wasn't even close, but the defending champion Seahawks figure to present a much tougher test as the Pats aim to halt a two-game losing streak while vying for the Lombardi Trophy.

Once again, Brady (23-of-35, 226 yards, three touchdowns, interception) was aided by a running back who eclipsed the century mark against a soft Colts defense front, as LeGarrette Blount bulldozed his way for 148 yards and three touchdowns on a franchise playoff record 30 carries to secure a date with the champs.

"It doesn't matter who we were going to play against," Blount said. "We're going to go out there and play against anybody, no matter if it's the defending champs or whoever. We're just going to go out there and play against anybody."

After a 31-point concession to the Ravens in the playoff opener, the Patriots defense righted the ship against Luck (12-of-33, 126 yards, two interceptions), the league's leader in touchdown passes. Cornerback Darrelle Revis dotted the exclamation point with a third-quarter interception that brought back memories of Ty Law, who watched part of the game on the Pats sideline. Revis also had a pass breakup on his only other target, and his performance proved vital against a series of assignments after the Patriots lost former top corner Aqib Talib to injuries in their previous pair of defeats in the conference title game.

The Patriots jumped out to an early lead and polished off the blowout in the second half, having outscored Luck's Colts, 189-73, in four meetings, including a 113-27 margin in the second half.

Brady shook off a scoreless opening possession, and the Pats took advantage of Josh Cribbs' muffed punt to grab an early lead. The Patriots took over at the Colts 24, and Blount's 1-yard plunge made it 7-0 six plays later.

Adam Vinatieri, who has made all kinds of big-time kicks in ugly weather conditions in Foxboro, shanked a 51-yard field goal attempt on the ensuing drive. Brady punctuated the error by delivering a 1-yard touchdown to fullback James Develin, who busted through a tackle to make it 14-0 late in the first quarter.

Brady momentarily let the Colts off the hook early in the second quarter when he

Patriots tight end Rob Gronkowski spikes the ball after a TD as wide receiver Danny Amendola looks on.
By Nancy Lane / Boston Herald

Indianapolis Colts quarterback Andrew Luck crawls off
the turf after throwing an interception to Patriots
cornerback Darrelle Revis in the third quarter.
By Matt West / Boston Herald

forced a throw into double coverage for tight end
Rob Gronkowski, and linebacker D'Qwell Jackson
intercepted the bid at the 1-yard line. The Colts
followed by showing their only offensive spark of
the night, and Zurlon Tipton's 1-yard touchdown
run cut it to 14-7 with 4:54 remaining in the half.
But Stephen Gostkowski's 21-yard field goal
extended the lead to 17-7 with 9 seconds to go.

The game got out of hand from there. After a
series of tackle-eligible plays, which have been a
staple all season, the Pats unveiled another
wrinkle when Brady dumped off a short pass to
left tackle Nate Solder, who stormed ahead for a
16-yard touchdown to make it 24-7 on the opening
drive of the third quarter.

"When I heard it called, I said, 'That's a great
call because it's going to work,' " Solder said.

After Luck's next three-and-out, Brady and
Gronkowski finally made one count with a 5-yard

scoring connection. Gronkowski beat cornerback
Greg Toler on a slant to make it 31-7. Revis
peeled off his assignment on the next series to
jump Luck's pass for receiver T.Y. Hilton, and he
returned it 30 yards to the Colts 13. Blount
scored on the next play to erase any doubt by
pushing the lead to 38-7, and he added a 2-yard
touchdown run in the fourth quarter to close the
scoring.

"It feels great," said receiver Julian Edelman,
who led the Pats with nine catches for 98 yards.
"It's an unbelievable feeling, but there's still one
more game." ∎

Patriots defensive end Zach Moore, right, celebrates with outside linebacker Jamie Collins after his interception.

By Matt West / Boston Herald

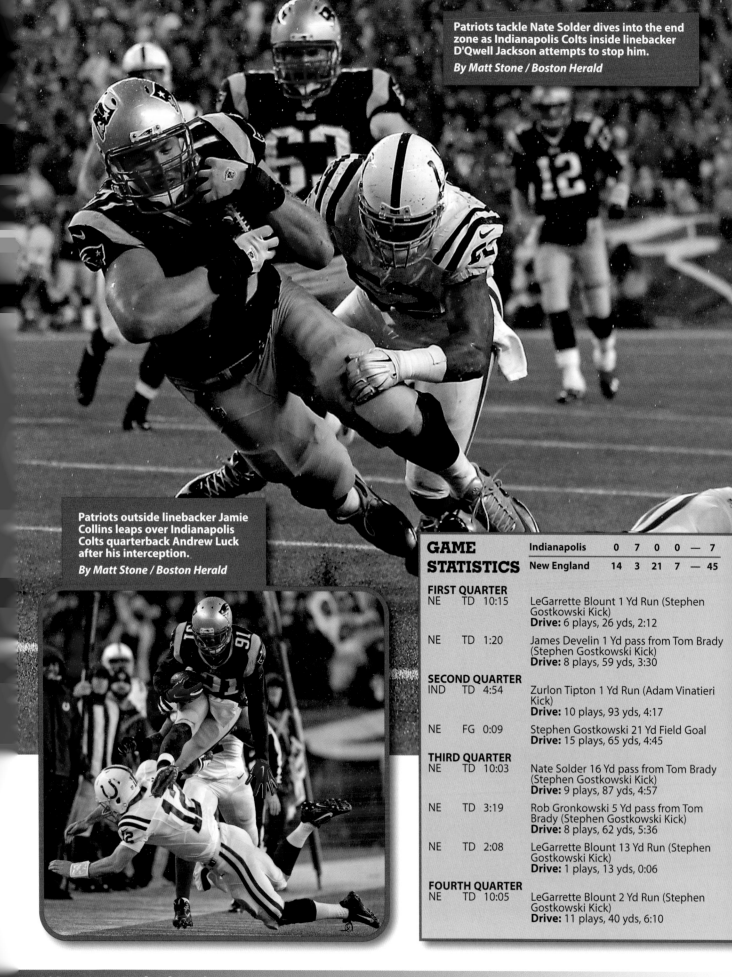

Patriots tackle Nate Solder dives into the end zone as Indianapolis Colts inside linebacker D'Qwell Jackson attempts to stop him.

By Matt Stone / Boston Herald

Patriots outside linebacker Jamie Collins leaps over Indianapolis Colts quarterback Andrew Luck after his interception.

By Matt Stone / Boston Herald

GAME STATISTICS

	Indianapolis	0	7	0	0	—	7
	New England	14	3	21	7	—	45

FIRST QUARTER

NE   TD   10:15   LeGarrette Blount 1 Yd Run (Stephen Gostkowski Kick)
Drive: 6 plays, 26 yds, 2:12

NE   TD   1:20   James Develin 1 Yd pass from Tom Brady (Stephen Gostkowski Kick)
Drive: 8 plays, 59 yds, 3:30

SECOND QUARTER

IND   TD   4:54   Zurlon Tipton 1 Yd Run (Adam Vinatieri Kick)
Drive: 10 plays, 93 yds, 4:17

NE   FG   0:09   Stephen Gostkowski 21 Yd Field Goal
Drive: 15 plays, 65 yds, 4:45

THIRD QUARTER

NE   TD   10:03   Nate Solder 16 Yd pass from Tom Brady (Stephen Gostkowski Kick)
Drive: 9 plays, 87 yds, 4:57

NE   TD   3:19   Rob Gronkowski 5 Yd pass from Tom Brady (Stephen Gostkowski Kick)
Drive: 8 plays, 62 yds, 5:36

NE   TD   2:08   LeGarrette Blount 13 Yd Run (Stephen Gostkowski Kick)
Drive: 1 plays, 13 yds, 0:06

FOURTH QUARTER

NE   TD   10:05   LeGarrette Blount 2 Yd Run (Stephen Gostkowski Kick)
Drive: 11 plays, 40 yds, 6:10

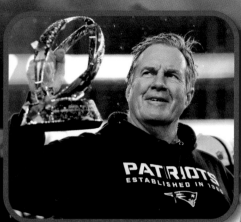

Patriots owner, Robert Kraft, far left, head coach Bill Belichick, left, and quarterback Tom Brady, below, celebrate with the Lamar Hunt trophy after the game.

By Nancy Lane / Boston Herald (far left, below)

By Matt West / Boston Herald (left)

A.J. Colarusso is 'pumped' for his first Super Bowl as the Patriots take on the Seahawks in Arizona.

By Matt West / Boston Herald

Pats fan Mike Perciballi of Toronto, CA with Pat Patriot at a pep rally in Phoenix.

By Nancy Lane / Boston Herald

Nadia Gaytan, a Pats fan from Mexico, gets ready to watch the Super Bowl.
By John Wilcox / Boston Herald

Patriots defensive tackle Vince Wilfork
celebrates after Malcolm Butler sealed
the game with a fourth-quarter
interception.
By Matt West / Boston Herald

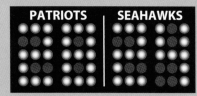

PATRIOTS   SEAHAWKS

JUST LIKE OLD TIMES

Brady leads Pats to 4th NFL title

By JEFF HOWE | *Boston Herald*

On to the White House.

The Patriots beat the Seattle Seahawks, 28-24, last night to win Super Bowl XLIX after Tom Brady's latest legacy drive and Malcolm Butler's last-minute miracle interception. The Pats, who won their fourth Super Bowl in franchise history in dramatic fashion by erasing a 24-14 fourth-quarter deficit, felt vindicated after two weeks of heat over football air pressure.

"Tell them to deflate this," Brandon Browner yelled to Vince Wilfork.

Brady completed all nine pass attempts for 72 yards and a 3-yard touchdown to Julian Edelman, who beat Tharold Simon for the score that gave the Patriots the four-point lead with 2:02 left to play.

"Considering the fact that I almost had like two heart attacks, it was still great," Edelman said of the wild fourth quarter. "It just shows once again how mentally tough this football team is. You knew it was going to be a special group from day one."

The 37-year-old Brady joined Joe Montana and Terry Bradshaw as the only quarterbacks to win four Super Bowls, and he became a three-time Super Bowl MVP while breaking a Super Bowl record with 37 completions on 50 attempts for 328 yards, four touchdowns and two interceptions.

"It's been a long journey," Brady said.

And for a defense that was constructed to better complement an offense after giving up the fourth-quarter lead in the team's previous two Super Bowl losses, it

Patriots fans Dean Martin and son Tim Martin of Arizona high five Gronk & Brady heads promoting Comcast Sports Network.

By Matt Stone / Boston Herald

Patriots quarterback Tom Brady hands off to running back LaGarette Blount.

By Nancy Lane / Boston Herald

Seattle Seahawks running back Marshawn Lynch is tackled by Patriots defensive end Rob Ninkovich and outside linebacker Dont'a Hightower.

By John Wilcox / Boston Herald

was Butler who played the hero role by intercepting Russell Wilson's end zone attempt from the 1-yard line with 20 seconds to play. Butler, who broke up a pass earlier in the drive, was inserted into the lineup late in the second half for the combination of Kyle Arrington and Logan Ryan.

"It's no question, we feel like we're the best (defense) in the league," Darrelle Revis said. "I don't know what the numbers are or where we rank, but this is the biggest game, the biggest stage and we won. We definitely won."

The Seahawks briefly suffocated the Patriots after the teams emerged from halftime tied, 14-14. The undrafted Chris Matthews, who had never caught an NFL pass before hauling in four throws for 109 yards and a touchdown last night, beat Arrington for 45 yards to the Pats 17-yard line on the opening drive of the third quarter. Rob

Ninkovich saved the drive with a third-and-1 stop of Marshawn Lynch for no gain, but Steven Hauschka's 27-yard field goal gave the Seahawks their first lead, 17-14.

Brady's bid for Rob Gronkowski on the ensuing drive was off target, and Bobby Wagner's pick set up the Seahawks at midfield. Wilson finished the job with an assist from an official, who picked Revis in the end zone and allowed Doug Baldwin to break free for a 3-yard touchdown catch to pad the lead, 24-14, with 4:54 remaining in the third quarter.

But the Patriots, who have only allowed 12 fourth-quarter points in their last nine games, shut it down again by holding the Seahawks scoreless in their final four possessions. The Seahawks surrendered 14 fourth-quarter points after allowing 13 total in their previous eight games.

"That's pretty awesome," Revis said of the way

Patriots tight end Rob Gronkowski pulls in a touchdown pass.
By Matt West / Boston Herald

Wide receiver Brandon LaFell crosses the goal line to put the Patriots up 7-0.

By John Wilcox / Boston Herald

the Pats have closed games. "I think it's the fight that we have. When we were down by 10 points, nobody ever pointed the finger at anybody. Nobody got down. We just got poised. We have great leadership on this team."

Brady only completed four passes in the third quarter after setting a Super Bowl record with 20 first-half completions, but he was sharp on a dire fourth-quarter drive. Edelman withstood a wicked hit from Kam Chancellor for a 21-yard gain on third-and-14 and added 21 more yards on a third-and-8 grab. Brady then delivered a missile to a leaping Danny Amendola for a 4-yard score to cut the deficit to 24-21 with 7:55 remaining.

The Patriots' first scoring opportunity ended when Brady was sandwiched by Michael Bennett and Cliff Avril while lofting an ill-fated third-and-6 pass toward a covered Edelman, and Jeremy Lane intercepted the underthrown ball in the end zone.

Lane, however, appeared to break his arm on the return, and Brady exposed his replacement, Simon, on the ensuing possession in the second quarter. Edelman beat Simon on an under route for 23 yards on third-and-10. Two plays later, the Pats opened the scoring when Brandon LaFell cut through Simon for an 11-yard touchdown on a slant route that gave the Pats a 7-0 lead.

"That's a great football team," Edelman said. "They didn't come back to the Super Bowl by accident. You tip your hat to the Seattle Seahawks. They made a lot of great plays. We were just fortunate to make a few more."∎

Patriots cornerback Logan Ryan and
Seattle Seahawks wide receiver
Jermaine Kearse battle for a pass.

By John Wilcox / Boston Herald

Seattle Seahawks running back
Marshawn Lynch gets some extra yards
as the Patriot defense takes him down.
By Matt Stone / Boston Herald

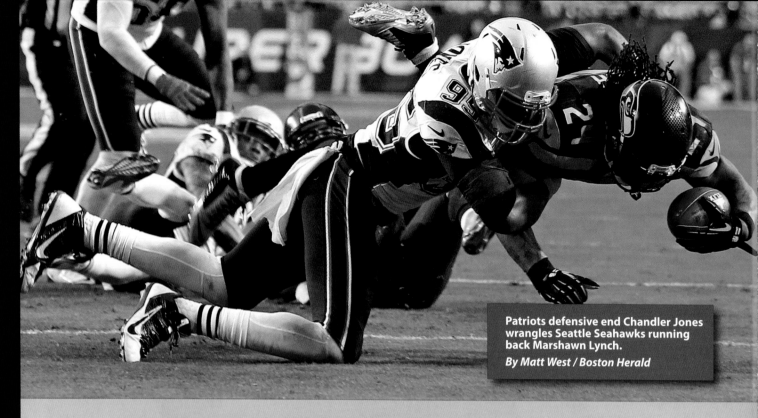

Patriots defensive end Chandler Jones wrangles Seattle Seahawks running back Marshawn Lynch.
By Matt West / Boston Herald

THE WEAKEST THINK

Pats make plays after Seahawks make gaffe

By RON BORGES | *Boston Herald*

Players win games. Coaches lose them. Malcolm Butler, who one moment earlier seemed to have become the Patriots' latest victim of The Curse of University of Phoenix Stadium, intercepted perhaps the most ill-advised pass in Super Bowl history at the goal line late last night and the Patriots had won their fourth Super Bowl of the century, defeating the Seattle Seahawks, 28-24, in Super Bowl XLIX.

Players make plays. Coaches make mistakes.

The Patriots had caught football's stingiest defense from behind, overcoming a 10-point deficit to take the lead with 122 seconds to go, then boom, boom and Seattle was at the Pats 5-yard line, first-and-goal with 66 seconds to play after a miraculous catch by Jermaine Kearse when a pass bounced off Butler's hand and then Kearse's legs, lap and fingers before he pulled it in on his back.

The haunting memory of David Tyree catching a football against his helmet in this same stadium eight years ago to save the Giants and ultimately help beat an undefeated Patriots team trying to make history crept into the minds of every fan who ever wore red, white and blue face paint in New England.

Tom Brady was seen saying "Oh, no," as he stared incredulously at the scoreboard video screen, that ball rattling around between Kearse's legs before he finally corralled it 33 yards from the line of scrimmage and 5 yards from the goal line.

Then cantankerous Marshawn Lynch nearly bulled his way in and everyone in the stadium knew what was coming. With the clock winding down to 26 seconds it would be Lynch again thrusting himself like a battering ram at the tiring Patriots defense with the ball sitting inside the 1-yard line. Who could stop him?

Patriots wide receiver Danny
Amendola catches his TD.
By Matt West / Boston Herald

Patriots defensive back Malcolm Butler makes the game-winning interception against Seahawks receiver Ricardo Lockette in the waning seconds of Super Bowl XLIX.

By Matt Stone / Boston Herald

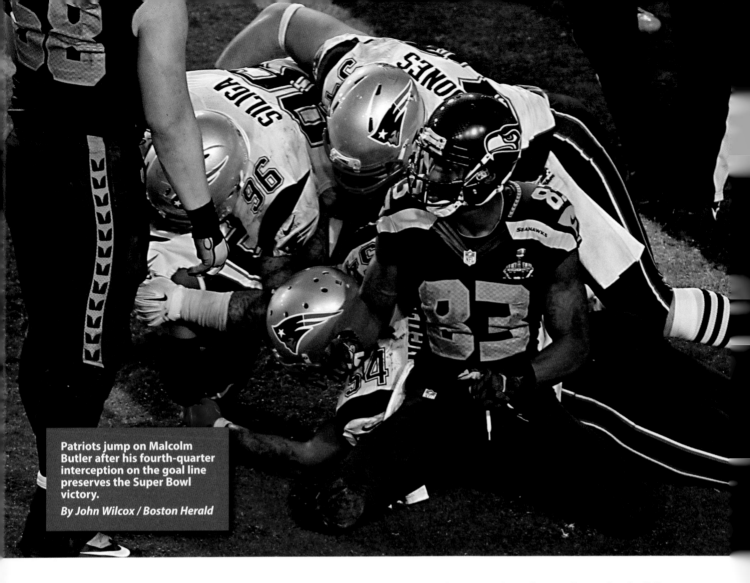

Patriots jump on Malcolm Butler after his fourth-quarter interception on the goal line preserves the Super Bowl victory.

By John Wilcox / Boston Herald

Only one man.

Players play. Coaches overthink.

Seahawks offensive coordinator Darrell Bevell decided at that point to turn a fifth-grade science project into the Manhattan Project.

Everyone knew the ball would be slammed into Lynch's belly and he would slam into the Patriots defense trying to gain his 103rd yard of the game. But a coach decided to take the ball out of the hands of the players and prove how fertile his mind could be.

Bevell incredibly called a pick play, asking Russell Wilson to complete a pass in the tightness of the goal line when all that had to be done was to plunge forward with football's most powerful running back. Butler read the play perfectly.

"At this time it seems like overthinking, but they have goal line guys on, we have three wide receivers, a tight end and one back," Seattle coach Pete Carroll said. "They've got extra guys at the line of scrimmage, so we don't want to waste a run play at that.

"It was a clear thought, but it didn't work out

right. We happened to throw them the ball."

Maybe it wasn't a clear thought, after all? Why not call timeout and settle down? And why were three wide receivers in with the ball inside the 1 when you're a power team?

Whatever the reasons, Butler saw the pick coming, got inside it and intercepted the ball as well as the Seahawks' dream of becoming the first team to repeat as Super Bowl champions since the Patriots did it 10 years ago.

"I just had a vision I was going to make a big play and it came true," said Butler. "I can't explain it now."

Surely neither can Bevell, who made the most boneheaded call in Super Bowl history, snatching defeat from the jaws of victory as Lynch stood staring in bewilderment, the disgusted look he usually reserves for a reporter's questions painted across his face.

The Butler did it, but so did a coach who refused to let his players decide the game. Bonehead, thy name is Bevell.

At halftime, Bill Belichick, a coach who would

have known better, told NBC's Michele Tafoya: "This is a players' game. Whichever players play best in the second half will win."

He was right, as he so often is when coaching instincts are involved. Belichick let his players play the entire game. Carroll did not and so, just as Belichick had predicted, a player decided it — his.

Had Bevell thought to do the same and handed the ball to Lynch once or twice more, it is difficult to imagine he would have been stopped by the exhausted Pats defense. But Bevell did not trust his best player enough. He tried instead to prove games like this are won by coaches.

Those players had slugged it out all night, each taking crushing blows only to recover and deliver ones of their own.

They were the best two teams in football and they proved it. Each had the opportunity to take the other out, but could not do it, not through any fault of their own but because their opponent was as resilient as they were.

Patriots tight end Rob Gronkowski lets fans touch the Lombardi Trophy as Tom Brady talks with owner Robert Kraft after beating the Seattle Seahawks in Super Bowl XLIX.

By Matt Stone / Boston Herald

Stubborn refusal to relent is a powerful weapon in the hands of skilled and gifted athletes. Last night, it was more important than the mind of Brady or the legs of Lynch. It was more valuable than the quickness of Michael Bennett or the strength of Vince Wilfork.

Super Bowl XLIX was decided by many things, but none more so than stubborn refusal to give in. That applied to both teams as they tore at each other play after play, quarter after quarter, the lead drifting back and forth, no one quite able to secure it until Butler did.

There were big plays from those you'd expect, like Brady and Wilson, like Lynch and Rob Gronkowski. And there were plays from an unknown Chris Matthews, who had been working in a sporting goods store until the Seahawks called and he ended up making his first NFL catches in the Super Bowl, four of them for 109 yards and a touchdown.

And of course there was Butler, as well as a coach who is far better known this morning than he would like. A coach who forgot the game belongs to the players.

Julian Edelman had just torched a fourth-string defensive back named Tharold Simon with an in-and-out move with 2:02 to play and the ball at the Seattle 3. He beat this tortured backup with the same move he'd beaten him with on a critical third-down play earlier, faking inside and then turning out and hauling in a rifle shot from Brady to take a 28-24 lead with only 122 seconds separating the Patriots from their fourth Super Bowl title since the turn of the century.

And then, in the final moments, the Seattle players made two big plays to counter that one and the ball sat inside the 1-yard line when a coach took the game away from those players and Malcolm Butler took the Lombardi Trophy away from the Seahawks and brought it home to New England.∎

GAME STATISTICS

	New England	0	14	0	14	—	28
	Seattle	0	14	10	0	—	24

SECOND QUARTER

NE TD 9:47 — Brandon LaFell 11 Yd pass from Tom Brady (Stephen Gostkowski Kick)
Drive: 9 plays, 65 yds, 4:10

SEA TD 2:16 — Marshawn Lynch 3 Yd Run (Steven Hauschka Kick)
Drive: 8 plays, 70 yds, 4:51

NE TD 0:31 — Rob Gronkowski 22 Yd pass from Tom Brady (Stephen Gostkowski Kick)
Drive: 8 plays, 80 yds, 1:45

SEA TD 0:02 — Chris Matthews 11 Yd pass from Russell Wilson (Steven Hauschka Kick)
Drive: 5 plays, 80 yds, 0:29

THIRD QUARTER

SEA FG 11:09 — Steven Hauschka 27 Yd Field Goal
Drive: 7 plays, 72 yds, 3:51

SEA TD 4:54 — Doug Baldwin 3 Yd pass from Russell Wilson (Steven Hauschka Kick)
Drive: 6 plays, 50 yds, 3:13

FOURTH QUARTER

NE TD 7:55 — Danny Amendola 4 Yd pass from Tom Brady (Stephen Gostkowski Kick)
Drive: 9 plays, 68 yds, 4:15

NE TD 2:02 — Julian Edelman 3 Yd pass from Tom Brady (Stephen Gostkowski Kick)
Drive: 10 plays, 64 yds, 4:50

Team Stat Comparison	NE	SEA
1st Downs	25	20
Passing 1st downs	21	10
Rushing 1st downs	1	8
1st downs from penalties	3	2
3rd down efficiency	8-14	3-10
4th down efficiency	0-0	0-0
Total Plays	72	53
Total Yards	377	396
Yards per play	5.2	7.5
Total Drives	12	11
Passing	320	234
Comp-Att	37-50	12-21
Yards per pass	6.3	9.8
Interceptions thrown	2	1
Sacks-Yards Lost	1-8	3-13
Rushing	57	162
Rushing Attempts	21	29
Yards per rush	2.7	5.6
Red Zone (Made-Att)	3-4	3-5
Penalties	5-36	7-70
Turnovers	2	1
Fumbles lost	0	0
Interceptions thrown	2	1
Defensive / Special Teams TDs	0	0
Possession	33:46	26:14

Left: Brandon Bolden, Timothy Wright and Jonathan Casillas with the the Lombardi Trophy.

Right: Patriots head coach Bill Belichick hugs his children after the win.

By Nancy Lane / Boston Herald

New England Patriots hoist the Lombardi Trophy after beating the Seahawks in the Super Bowl.

By Matt West / Boston Herald